# Stranger Things
# and Philosophy

T0151363

# Popular Culture and Philosophy®   Series Editor: George A. Reisch

**For full details of all Popular Culture and Philosophy® books, visit www.opencourtbooks.com.**

Popular Culture and Philosophy®

# *Stranger Things* and Philosophy

*Thus Spake the Demogorgon*

EDITED BY

JEFFREY A. EWING AND

ANDREW M. WINTERS

OPEN COURT
Chicago

*Volume 126 in the series, Popular Culture and Philosophy®, edited by George A. Reisch*

**To find out more about Open Court books, visit our website at www.opencourtbooks.com**.

Open Court Publishing Company is a division of Carus Publishing Company, dba Cricket Media.

Copyright © 2019 by Carus Publishing Company, dba Cricket Media

First printing 2019

*Stranger Things and Philosophy: Thus Spake the Demogorgon*

This book has not been prepared, authorized, or endorsed by the creators or producers of *Stranger Things*.

**ISBN: 978-0-8126-9470-3**

**Library of Congress Control Number: 2019948499**

This book is also available as an e-book (ISBN 978-0-8126-9474-1)

*Andrew: For Moleek, PA D&D Buddies, and my Strange Students (you know who you are).*

*Jeffrey: To Kadie, for always putting me right-side up when I'm stranded in the Upside Down. You're always everything I need.*

# Contents

## Contents

# Thanks

This project could not have begun without the assistance of David Ramsay Steele and George Reisch at Open Court.

Thank you to our families, friends, and students who have suffered through numerous conversations about *Stranger Things* and all the strange things that we have analyzed.

Thank you to the group of students in the Philosophy of Science Fiction course at Slippery Rock University of Pennsylvania, where we had an opportunity to discuss the show in the context of reading philosophy.

Thank you to the chapter authors who helped us better understand *Stranger Things* and prepared pieces that we could not have imagined—that's a good thing.

Andrew also wants to thank Jonathan Thorn for helping him think about the nature of plastic.

# How to Make Something Strange Even Stranger

ANDREW M. WINTERS

Welcome to *Stranger Things and Philosophy*! The show has swept the nation, older and younger generations alike. Those of us who enjoyed much of the Eighties huddled over tables playing Dungeons & Dragons, using our imaginations to entertain ourselves and our friends, find a nostalgic delight in the throwback references to a vanished time.

For myself, there's still something comfortable about being serenaded by the delightful 8-bit sounds of NES video games. Both Nintendo and SEGA have capitalized on the rereleases of their 1980s devices and there are plenty of composers who specialize in 8-bit compositions. But what makes people so hungry to return to a time that was so plastic? Plastic TV trays to hold plastic TV dinners, while families sat on plastic couch covers. Consumerism was rampant and even the toys of that time were mostly plastic devices stamped with "Made in China."

While we saw ourselves being drawn to a plastic world, we found ourselves drawn to a malleable world—a world in which we, too, dreamed that we could become something new. It was a time of hope, despite wars and economic systems that never trickled down far enough. More importantly, it was a time of storytelling in which we viewed ourselves as the author, protagonist, and narrator wrapped in one. It was a time of creation. What better material than plastic to create something new?

But this would only explain why those of us who were alive during the Eighties would be attracted to a show that so closely attempts to mimic some of our favorite memories. What about those who weren't even dreamt of yet? I don't have the answer. Perhaps you can tell me, but if I had to speculate, the current culture is even more quick. There's currently no time to develop a thoroughgoing narrative that encapsulates a well-developed plot line. Those things that have the capacity of doing so are anachronistic—they've somehow escaped the present.

Instead of consuming plastic, we consume information. A world that was once driven by 8-bit entertainment has been dwindled to the single bit tweets, notifications, and snaps . . . or whatever else is out there. Our meaning is no longer tied to overarching stories, but, instead, we find meaning in the single like. We look to others for our confirmation. Instead we should be creating worlds together. To paraphrase Edward Norton's unnamed character from Fight Club, we should be more than single-serving friends to both each other and ourselves. We should treat ourselves as being more than single or 8-bit objects. We deserve more thorough descriptions than those that can be reduced to zeroes and ones.

So, I would claim that the show *Stranger Things* benefits both those who remember the Eighties and those who wish they remembered the Eighties. For those of us who were around, it reminds us of the world we left behind—the friendships, the adventures, and the abilities to go outside at night on your bike without the electronic tether of a cell phone (the only form of communication a child should have is a walkie-talkie).

For those of you who don't recall the 1980s, *Stranger Things* offers you a glimpse of a world in which you were given freedom to create your own story, instead of being given a fabricated silicone dream. (Even books allowed us to choose our own adventures.) Most importantly, it was a time when friends didn't lie. Unfortunately, now, we spend the majority of the time deceiving each other—only showing each other highlights as we hide behind Instagram filters.

I'm not a Luddite by any means. Technology has the capacity to save lives, lead to democracy, and bring us together—even those of us who might never meet IRL. Instead, I'm in love with a story—a narrative that indicates that our lives are more dynamic than the static digital world would have us believe. This is what *Stranger Things* offers us, a chance to see that we can use our imaginations to discover the joyous and the horrible. It's an inspiring story that offers us a chance to see what our friendships could be like. So, while the show is certainly entertaining and offers an aesthetically pleasing and horrifying experience from the opening sequence, there are so many additional layers to explore in the show.

In attempting to better understand the multifaceted nature of *Stranger Things*, the contributors explore philosophical issues that underly the show's themes. The topics the authors explore include the nature of horror and why we love to entertain ourselves with things that frighten us or revolt us; the importance of friendship and the underlying agreements we make by being a friend; what makes something a monster and whether or not all monsters are evil; the aesthetic unpleasantness of the ugliness that is found in the Upside Down; the extent to which the members of the Party might have a responsibility to disobey their adult guardians; how something like an Eggo can be a motivator for saving the world; the role of nostalgia and how maybe it is sometimes better to forget; how the Shadow Monster may not just be something found in the world, but is something we find in ourselves; how Will Byers's being possessed by the Mind Flayer calls into question our own personal and social identities; how an entire social movement behind a dead fictitious character can teach us to be more compassionate towards those who really need our help; how our understanding of the strange and abnormal can make us proud to be freaks; how horror can teach us how to be better humans; how something that may be an invasive species might actually be worth preserving; that the Mind Flayer may help us understand the nature of the divine; and how Eleven's heroism can offer us guidance on how to live a more meaningful life.

While the show *Stranger Things* is certainly strange, it becomes even that much more strange when you add a little philosophy to the mix. Like Dante following Virgil through the levels of Hell, we should follow Mike, Will, Lucas, Dustin, Eleven, and Maxine through the layers of *Stranger Things* to better understand the nature of reality, knowledge, morality, beauty, and ourselves.

We hope that this volume will allow you to view the show in a new way; have more conversations with your friends about the strange events and characters; and maybe learn a little philosophy along the way. Who knows, maybe this volume will get you to better appreciate the strangeness and value of philosophy. So, get a cup of coffee as you cuddle up with this book alongside a good friend. You may even want to do this first thing in the morning.

As Chief Hopper reminds us, "Mornings are for coffee and contemplation." We couldn't agree more.

# I

## Strange
## Thoughts

# 1
# Barb Dead, People Mad

ERIC HOLMES AND JEREMY CHRISTENSEN

Despite appearing in only the first three episodes of Season One before her death at the hands of the Demogorgon, Barb became a sensation, spawning an online social movement referred to as #JusticeForBarb. The #JusticeForBarb movement began soon after the show's debut on Netflix in the summer of 2016 and is an example of Internet Rage, wherein people demanded that the death of Barb be addressed by the fictional residents of fictional Hawkins, Indiana, and somehow rectified.

Unlike other online social movements that addressed serious issues such as totalitarianism (#The Arab Spring), police brutality and racial profiling (#BlackLivesMatter), or economic inequality (#Occupy Wall Street), #JusticeForBarb looked to avenge the death of a fictional character on a television show about interdimensional monsters.

Barb, kind, conscientious, loyal, and celibate, would have easily been the Final Girl if *Stranger Things* had been a slasher film of the 1980s, as her humility and loyalty would ensure that the likes of Freddy Krueger would never lay a knife-edged finger on her. However, given that she is killed only three episodes into Season One, *Stranger Things* treats Barb as little more than a plot device and that (along with some social trends to be discussed in the rest of this chapter) is why #JusticeForBarb became a thing in the first place.

With social media as a daily part of contemporary life, it's easier than ever for social movements like #JeSuisCharlie or the Ice Bucket Challenge to quickly grow and spread around the nation, or even planet, and across different demographics. It's easy to see how the tools used for legitimate social movements could be taken and used for whimsical purposes. However, the passion behind #Justice-ForBarb shows that the lines between reality and fiction are blurring.

## Hyperreality in Hawkins

French philosopher Jean Baudrillard writes in his 1981 book *Simulacra and Simulation* that everything produced by people (including stories) exists in three historical periods. In the first period, stories were either oral (like around a campfire) or painstakingly produced by hand. In this stage, an oral story or a handwritten book was completely unique, even if it was a word-for-word reproduction of someone else's story or another book of stories (like the Bible). These stories were produced to convey some kind of truth and were irreplaceable, as they were completely unique in their creation and in the final state of being.

In the second period, because of the invention of movable type and printing presses, stories become mass-produced and a million copies of the same book could be identical. In the case of electronic media like *Stranger Things*, the copy and experience are infinitely reproducible and theoretically available for consumption to seven billion people an infinite number of times. This is what Baudrillard refers to as an endless "precession of simulacra" (*Simulacra and Simulation*, p. 1). He states that modern and postmodern periods are marked by this innovation of reproduction that makes it possible to separate the artist (the movie maker), the art (*Stranger Things*), and the audience (us) in such a way that the historical condition that gave rise to the story recedes from the artifact and loses its meaning.

That's not to say persons can't feel something for the artifact or that some individual reaction to a piece of work may not be heartfelt. Instead, Baudrillard believes that the mass production and reproduction of a story means that the historical issues that give rise to that story (such as class struggle, ethnic tensions, gender dynamics) get further removed from those historical issues and that real, felt, bonded human experiences in face-to-face communities (like sitting around a campfire) disappear.

In the first order of simulacrum, a story would get reworked and be retold with new character names or even new locations. Storytellers would add their own style or a mark of the historical present in which the narrative was told. Because of this, the story would offer some uniqueness even if the core plot remains the same. Once mass production became the standard, stories became largely locked in place and the mechanical work of dissemination (along with copyright laws) ensured that stories became forever cemented rather than being retold.

Homage, the process of borrowing from the works of others to assemble the appearance of something new, becomes the only way for something new to be available. The sanctity of the original copy is gone, as it can always be replaced by one of the many exact copies that exist. Stories become easily disposable which, while not taking away from the efforts made to produce them, makes them much easier for the audience to discard, as they can easily be replaced.

In the third period, stories and reality become tangled and indistinguishable. This is what Baudrillard calls *hyperreality.* At this stage, reality and fiction fuse in such a way that fiction becomes real, or even "more real than the real" (p. 81). In the case of *Stranger Things,* the #Justice-ForBarb movement, as impassioned as it was, is a prime example of hyperreality in action.

## Barb and the "Meh" Triarchy

Barb's marginalization and victimization in *Stranger Things*, according to Baudrillard, offers a more real example of female disempowerment than someone like Jamie Haggard, as reported by Juliet Muir. Haggard, a twenty-seven-year-old mother of two from Washington state, went missing the same year that Season One of *Stranger Things* was released and her remains were recovered on the two-year anniversary of that release.

Haggard's disappearance and death, like the scores of other women who go missing annually, did not have a hashtag movement adopted in her name. Her disappearance and consequent death in the real world were met (except by Haggard's family and close friends) with the same sort of public indifference that Barb's disappearance and death was met with in Hawkins, which was an almost universal "meh."

Juxtaposed with that indifference is the real-world reaction to the death of Barb: a social media movement and tributes. Barb's death somehow allowed her to become more real and more important than other victims who lived in the real world and, in the case of *Stranger Things* and the #JusticeForBarb movement, this is where we currently find ourselves: fictional characters who suffer injustice are championed while living people suffering the same fate are ignored. In fact, more people care about Barb in the real world than in the fictional world of Hawkins and this is clear from the popularity of the Barb character and the indifference of the people of Hawkins toward Barb after her disappearance.

Art, in all its forms, has inspired activism; however, such artistically inspired activism turns toward making change in the world in which we all live. In the case of #JusticeForBarb, the process is reversed. Actual historical conditions—those that involve flesh and blood creatures operating in a finite and physical world—inspired efforts to find justice for a fictional person. Baudrillard, in his analysis of Disneyland, notes that it is the ultimate example of hyperreality and claims that it "is presented as imaginary in order to make us believe the rest is real, whereas all of Los Angeles and the America that surrounds it are no longer real, but belong to the hyperreal order and to the order of simulation" (p. 12).

By comparison, *Stranger Things* becomes a site, a place pilgrims travel to arrive at pure simulation, as it's devoid even of those imperfections like smell and heat that affect the human body at Disneyland; it is truly a place of escape. That is not unique. *Stranger Things* stands alongside hundreds of thousands of other fantasy novels, movies, and epic poems that offer similar places of escape.

What makes this case unique is that in this instance the audience sees danger in the show and believes it greater than the danger in the actual world that they live in. Jamie

Haggard, a flesh and blood person who was savagely murdered, becomes one of thousands whose sacrifice serves as an impetus to find justice for a fictional character. Whatever #JusticeForBarb represents for empowerment in the actual now serves as a movement to save the never dead because they were never really alive in the fictional world. But how does this inversion emerge?

## Buzzkill Barb

In Season One of *Stranger Things,* little attention is paid to the disappearance of Barb, as she's unpopular in school, plain in appearance, and studious, all of which are qualities that lead to anonymity. Barb, in Hawkins, is a buzzkill, a prop, a one-dimensional character easily discarded like a used tissue to advance the plot. In the real world, she became an icon and a cause to be championed and celebrated in both life and in death, as evidenced by the real-world candlelight vigil that was held to honor Barb's "life" on September 17th, 2016, in Malden, Massachusetts (reported by J.D. Capelouto). Barb, in the real world, is celebrated on T-shirts, in a mural in Los Angeles (graffiti found in Los Angeles, 2016), and even as inspiration for a pizza (as reported by D. Getz). Barb is a celebrity in the real-world and a zero in Hawkins.

Compare that to the response to the disappearance of Will Byers and you'll see that Barb's disposability stands out. Unlike Will, for whom the town musters support, including local law enforcement; a group of friends who band together and undertake to find him; a distraught and determined mother who pesters the town sheriff at every turn; and a brother who enlists the aid of the object of his desire.

Support for Barb, however, is thin at best and non-existent at worst. Passing references to Barb appear after the third episode, but the plot's focus and the characters' interest remain concentrated upon a single outcome: bringing Will home. Nancy makes efforts to find Barb, but, in Hawkins and in the living rooms of viewers worldwide, Will Byers and not Barb gets top billing on the missing child marquee. It is this lack of concern for Barb—a plain, quiet, young woman, rather than a plain, quiet, young boy—that is the cornerstone of the #JusticeForBarb movement, as viewers found it unacceptable that this young woman would be forsaken as she was.

Viewer consternation over this lack of concern for Barb's disappearance is what happens when real experience disappears. According to Baudrillard, people reinvent the real as fiction, believing that stories are facts (p. 45) and do this to substitute for the absence of an actual experience in daily life. After all, how often do we get to right a wrong and secure justice for a life taken too soon? How often do any of us go on an adventure? Most of our lives are lacking in genuine excitement and intrigue, so we seek it elsewhere.

Barb, as a character, is largely one-dimensional. While appearing in the first three episodes of Season One, Barb's scenes and dialogue are mostly limited to conversing with Nancy, most notably trying to convince her not to go to Steve Harrington's house and pointing out that she is wearing a new bra in the second episode. Barb argues to Nancy that Steve Harrington merely wants to seduce her and cares little for her. In short, Barb is a stock "good friend" but her disappearance and the failure of the authorities to take serious action makes her akin to Jamie Haggard and the plethora of other women who go missing in America every year, many of whom are largely ignored by law enforcement, especially if they are on the fringes of society. Her story, then, is a metaphor for those women, and #JusticeForBarb seeks to amend the failure of real justice for real women in the real world by finding justice for a fictional woman in a fictional world.

## You Get a Barb, and You Get a Barb, Every World Gets a Barb!

From Baudrillard's perspective, pleading the case for #JusticeForBarb is a way to secure true justice, one that seems impossible in the real world. Taking to the streets in Boston (or online) for Barb's sake becomes a way to avenge a misjustice, any misjustice, as #JeSuisCharlie failed to stop mass shootings, just as #BlackLivesMatter failed to stop police brutality, and just as #Kony2012 failed to stop the Lord's Resistance Army.

#JusticeForBarb is an intersection between the real and the fictional where well-intentioned people try to restore inside of a fictional world what was lost in the real world; in this particular case, justice for women like Jamie Haggard who disappeared and later were found to have been victims of violence. The dwindling of #JusticeForBarb as a movement not only coincided with the release of Season Two of *Stranger Things* in October 2017 (wherein Barb's disappearance is finally given the attention that her defenders craved), but also with the rise of #MeToo, a social movement that has had far reaching consequences and has ended many careers of alleged sexual predators who largely preyed on women.

The dismay in response to Barb's largely unnoticed death (in Hawkins at least) is an overreaction for certain (we're talking about fiction here, people) but is a clear sign of the passion and investment that people have in the stories that they enjoy and this adds to the continual blurring of the lines between fiction and reality. The actor who played Barb, Shannon Purser, herself acknowledged on ABC's *Jimmy Kimmel Live* in September 2018 (more than two years after the debut of *Stranger Things* and the consequent death of Barb in The Upside Down) that she is still referred to as "Barb" on a regular basis and that her own mother once called her by that name.

Even media outlets have a hard time distinguishing reality and fiction. An October 24th 2017 article on Refinery29 entitled *"Riverdale* Just Threatened to Kill Off Barb Again" complains about the prospect of Shannon Purser's character on *Riverdale* (an unrelated and also fictional television show) potentially being murdered by that show's second season villain, The Black Hood, as if Riverdale is the Upside Down and as if it even matters, that somehow a character played by Shannon Purser is inherently deserving to live in perpetuity. This isn't to say that the author of that particular article alone struggles to separate reality from fiction—our society does. American culture, one long built on mythologies like Manifest Destiny and the American Dream, is increasingly invested in stories of good and evil, of justice and injustice, of creating and maintaining a better world, which goes a long way toward understanding the vitriol in our modern politics.

## Eighties Ladies

With events that take place in the fictional world of Hawkins being reacted to in the real world, Baudrillard's simulacrum, his hyperreality, becomes real. *Stranger Things* follows the rules of hyperreality, as the show is a series of reproductions of other movies of the 1980s with slight modifications. To understand the series, viewers have to be detectives, making note of other earlier movies that are mimicked. The audience must participate in the process of the hyperreal, working to find the answer, to reveal not only plot but also to find the meaning of iconic images shown on screen and #Justice-forBarb is the logical extension of that pursuit.

The show offers a series of clues, not so much about what is unfolding for Will and his band of friends, but rather a series of clues about the 1980s movies that inspired *Stranger Things*. To truly view the show, the audience must be versed in its creators' love of the era and its science-fiction, horror, and teen movies. The series features a hodgepodge of images, lines, and plot structures borrowed from landmark science-fiction, horror, and teen films of the 1980s, from its Richard Greenberg–inspired opening credits sequence to its references to 1980s genre films like *E.T. the Extra-Terrestrial* and *Poltergeist*.

Whether it is the angst of one's child disappearing while still somehow being in your home (Joyce knows that Will is somehow present while physically missing, just as the Freeling family knows the same thing about Carol Anne in *Poltergeist*); Eleven getting a nosebleed while using tele-kinesis (just like Charlie McGee in *Firestarter*); or a rag-tag group of kids approaching their destiny atop BMX bicycles (as in *The Goonies*), *Stranger Things* borrows heavily from the era in which it is set. This is vital toward understanding just how #JusticeForBarb took ahold of the pop cultural zeitgeist in 2016.

The development of the show also borrows heavily from the 1980s. For example, while casting the show, *Stranger Things*'s creators, Matt and Ross Duffer, had those auditioning for the roles of Mike, Dustin, Lucas, and Will read lines from the 1986 film *Stand by Me*. Even the pitch that the Duffer brothers made to Netflix was comprised of clips and scores from 1980s genre films, including *Close Encounters of the Third Kind*, *A Nightmare on Elm Street,* and *Halloween*. The website Screen Daily quotes Matt Duffer as saying that, "It had movies like *E.T. the Extra-Terrestrial* but with a John Carpenter synth score on it . . . I watch it back now and it's pretty close to the show. The pitch was probably sixty percent accurate to what we ended up making" (Grater 2017).

The opening scene, for instance, establishes the framework for reading the series and provides a method for understanding justice as simulacrum through simulation. Borrowing from the opening scene in Steven Spielberg's *E.T. the Extra-Terrestrial*, which features four adolescents gathered around a dining table in a middle-class home playing Dungeons & Dragons, *Stranger Things* opens in the basement of a middle-class home featuring four adolescents playing the same game. Recreating this scene trains the audience to see the entire show as a kind of reality borrowed from their own moviegoing experience, but one that they can only understand if they have first encountered the original copy—*E.T. the Extra-Terrestrial*.

On the one hand, a person who grew up without watching science-fiction, horror, and teen films from the 1980s can certainly appreciate *Stranger Things* as a series, a hero's journey, or a junior romp adventure fest. However, full engagement with the show through understanding its codes requires some investment in the works that inspired it.

Like understanding an ironic gesture, which requires first an understanding of what is being critiqued before getting the joke of the critique, truly appreciating *Stranger Things* requires that viewers understand the history of the genres and the stories that it draws from. Viewers have to comb through the dialogue, costumes, sets, and plot to find its full meaning. From there, the detective work begins by finding pieces of the past just like a cultural archeologist would. However, there is one particular artifact that plays the most essential role in understanding the rise of #JusticeForBarb: Dungeons & Dragons.

## Dungeons and Dragons and Duffers, Oh My!

#JusticeforBarb expresses the hyperreal nature of the audience's relationship to the show, as they feel they are part of the game they're told to play; they serve (or believe they do) as the dungeon masters for the plot and outcome of the program. Central to understanding *Stranger Things* is the roleplaying game Dungeons & Dragons, which exploded in popularity in the 1980s. The first premise an audience must accept to invest in *Stranger Things* is that role playing is reality. The four preteens in Mike Wheeler's basement playing Dungeons & Dragons fuse with an actual Dungeons & Dragons adventure. Their unreal becomes real, as the monster that they try to defeat is referred to as a Demogorgon, which is the same name that is assigned to the monster from The Upside Down that eventually captures Will.

As in the game, each character of the tight-knit group must use his or her powers, find valuable talismans, enlist the aid of mentors, and avoid or defeat a host of fantastic creatures in order to reach their goal: the return of one of their band to the fold. Simultaneously, yet inversely, the unreal of *Stranger Things* becomes the real for the audience. Just like Lucas, Mike, Dustin, and Eleven seek to rescue Will, supporters of #JusticeForBarb embark on their own mission to rescue Barb from injustice. In this, the injustice is the writer's room who allowed Barb to be dismissed as part of the guild in the first place. #JusticeForBarb can't undo Barb's death, but it can at least give her some dignity in death.

In Hawkins, those who are successful at role play can find justice; likewise then, those audience members who understand the map of *Stranger Things* can also, they believe, find justice. As Baudrillard states,

> Today's abstraction is no longer that of the map, the double, the mirror, or the concept. Simulation is no longer that of a territory, a referential being, or a substance. It is the generation by models of a real without origin or reality: a hyperreal. (Simulacra and Simulation, p. 1)

Barb, who appeared in the original quest only to be devoured, is then resurrected by a core group of fans who seek to extend her journey and thereby control the game. Dungeons & Dragons perfectly presents the legend for reading *Stranger Things* as an imperative to find something. Here, in the dungeons of Hawkins and the Upside Down, a motley band with various powers engages in a quest to recover Will. Unlike explorers of the past, the map in the roleplaying game is not any actual territory. Nothing real needs to exist except an imaginary world which takes place in the mind and a suspension of disbelief, a practice necessary to making sense of the world of the hyperreal.

*Stranger Things* creates the illusion of active audience participation in the outcomes via the process that urges viewers to search for Easter eggs, ephemera, and other artifacts from 1980s popular culture. Critically, the show features Dungeons & Dragons prominently as a means to read the show and it is more than a fun throwback to the era. Dungeons & Dragons, as a game, is played on graph paper and that familiar grid of squares appears nearly everywhere in *Stranger Things*. The hallways in the Hawkins Lab? Grid. Shirts worn by Will, Barb, Nancy, and Mrs. Wheeler (amongst others)? Grids. The wallpaper in Steve Harrington's bedroom? Grid. Even Eleven's beloved Eggo waffles contain a grid pattern. The grid pattern is so prevalent in the design of *Stranger Things* that it can't be happenstance. It's an invitation to see the entirety of the series as a gameboard. Just like The Upside Down, it's all around you but you have to be able to see it.

If *Stranger Things* is a game, its primary quest is to save Will. However, like an expansion pack, #JusticeForBarb is an add on that viewers took it upon themselves to create. Like an Upside Down version of an alternate reality game, supporters of #JusticeForBarb took it upon themselves to use the activism tools of our world to find justice for the untimely death of a fictional woman in another world. Our world and the worlds created in writers' rooms are blurring to the point of being indistinguishable from one another.

## Eleven Is a Teen Witch

Baudrillard explains that hyperreality exists when fiction and reality intertwine so that they are indistinguishable. The constant references to scenes in other movies, camera angles, and even lines of dialogue reveal that those fictional places are the real history of the hyperreality. The entirety of *Stranger Things* works by representing images from 1980s pop culture as the ground for the historical real, in accordance with Baudrillard's account of the hyperreal: "As one image intersects with another, it is the experience of image itself, not each image's unique voice, that defines what has happened" (p. 4).

By that logic, *Stranger Things* becomes the official history of the Eighties. Rather than a direct critique of problems in the 2010s, *Stranger Things*, by borrowing the images of 1980s movies, simply recycles problems and their critiques. The most obvious point of this development emerges in the military industrial complex sequences of the series. *E.T. the Extra-Terrestrial* featured this theme prominently during its 1982 release. Shadowy government figures were bent on tracking down innocent, private citizens, suspending all rights to ensure "national security."

In *Stranger Things,* that theme remains, but by 2016 the United States government's particular technologies of infiltrating the lives of private citizens have improved significantly. In the 1980s, military control and encroachment was pointed outward toward the Soviet Union. In the case of *E.T. the Extra-Terrestrial*, private citizens were the casualty of that war because they were protecting an outsider, a literal alien.

The means of controlling the population in the 1980s was by brute force, as there were no opportunities to insert malware onto personal computers or to surveil people's smartphones. Those practices have radically transformed the real relationship of the United States government to its citizens. *Stranger Things* ignores that change and instead recycles the conflicts of government control as purely physical, just like in the 1980s. Essentially, *Stranger Things* mutes the present, numbing it to real concerns in favor of trapping the images of conflict in a predictable past.

Further establishing this hyperreal historical provenance is the juxtaposition of Barb with Eleven, a montage heroine cut from the myth of 1980s movies, many of which are retellings of legends about Joan of Arc. Like Joan of Arc, Eleven demonstrates an exceptional power (clairvoyance) and seeks to dispel invading forces, although the Lovecraftian horrors of The Upside Down are far more grotesque than the English.

Like many 1980s films, most notably *E.T. the Extra-Terrestrial,* *Firestarter,* and *Teen Witch*, government incompetence, arrogance, and patriarchal authority seek to stop any power that threatens it, particularly androgynous forces (like E.T.) or women, as in the case of *Firestarter* or *Teen Witch*. Co-ordinated efforts, black-suited men (other than a token female agent in *Stranger Things*), people in hazmat suits, and a desire to quarantine and surveil capture the essence of the vast and mysterious authority.

Eleven, quarantined by that authority, uses her paranormal powers not only to escape but also to defeat those forces of surveillance by calling upon powers that exist outside of the real. Barb, on the other hand, possesses negligible power. For the most part, Barb succumbs to pressure from her friends, pressure that leads directly to her death. Barb's death is a direct result of Nancy's peer pressure, as Barb is pressured into going to Steve Harrington's in the first place, not to mention that she is pressured to shotgun a beer, which leads to the wound on her hand that draws the Demogorgon to her.

Barb is the avatar of every woman who has ever been victimized due to either the inability to defend herself, an unwillingness to stand up for herself, or the perception of being weak. Her plain dress, unfashionable glasses, and milquetoast demeanor show her as a representation of the generic everywoman, a drab fieldmouse of a person who is easily forgotten and thus ignored. Significantly, Barb lacks agency even in her own demise. Sitting peacefully on a diving board of a backyard pool, she lingers, trying not to intrude on Nancy's romantic encounter with Steve Harrington during "The Weirdo on Maple Street." As Barb waits, the Demogorgon consumes her, but the camera isn't even focused on her. The scene of her death is intercut with images of Nancy and Steve fooling around in an upstairs bedroom. Even in death at the hands of an interdimensional monster, Barb plays second fiddle to Nancy.

## Don't Worry Barb, We're Coming!

*Stranger Things* reinforces the message that the real is insufficient. Barb cannot save herself because what exists in reality is simply the illusion of power—obscurity creates insecurity—real force comes from that which abides only in fantasy. Eleven, whose abilities allow her to move inter-dimensionally, demonstrates the power of fusing fantasy and reality, destroying those distinctions. Barb, conversely, only exists in her reality and is so mired in it that she cannot conceive of engaging in bad behaviors such as teen sex, drinking, or defying her parents, let alone the possibility that a Demogorgon lurks beneath the placid surface of a suburban swimming pool.

Baudrillard writes that in the hyperreal "the feeling of the real, of the banal, of lived experience, will be to reinvent the real as fiction, precisely because it has disappeared from our life" (p. 124). Eleven and her fantastic power magnifies that banality on screen. #JusticeforBarb demonstrates it in actuality, as its participants operate like Eleven, shifting between the actual conditions of women's oppression and the fantastic world of oppression occupied by Barb.

#JusticeforBarb became that kind of supernatural force, something external to the reality in which Barb exists that forces itself into the *Stranger Things* story like a more powerful narrative that can come to her aid, much like Eleven's gift of telekinesis can flip vans and immobilize government agents. Protestors teleport through reality into fantasy to rescue her from the fate of being forgotten in death as she was in life. The '#', in this case, becomes a talisman, not unlike the boombox or lights that Will uses to communicate with Joyce while he is trapped in the Upside Down. This talisman pushes away the darkness and comes to the rescue of those who are under attack or, in the case of Barb, at least allows for justice to be served.

This time, the natural order of the real—or at least the hypertextual real of the Twitterverse—inserts itself into the fictional world, fusing the two orders at the site of injustice over Barb. Speaking as a voice from outside the narrative, a supreme judge that determines the right order of a universe, members of the #JusticeForBarb movement condemn the injustices of the world of Hawkins; however, their voices, their very presence is written out, as the fourth wall divides the concerned citizen from the world of fiction. Their narratives, at least in Season One, are not part of the script.

Like Greek gods, those concerned citizens descend from their Olympic seats into the world of simulated mortals because the injustice of that world impacts the justice of their world.

## Barb Is the World, Barb Is the Children

What occurs is a kind of holographic projection, if not in image but in sentiment, into the world of *Stranger Things*. Baudrillard claims that all television is a holographic projection, a form of technology that produces hyperreal "clones" of actual persons. As he writes (albeit densely),

> The hologram, the one of which we have always already dreamed (but these are only poor bricolages of it) gives us the feeling, the vertigo of passing to the other side of our own body, to the side of the double, luminous clone, or dead twin that is never born in our place, that watches over us in anticipation. (p. 106)

More directly, the fiction of pixels appears like us; the bodies look so real that they could be us and so we treat them like that. To this end, the intersection of the protesters in *Stranger Things* via their # conduit offers no inconsistency in the hyperreal; Barb is their twin or even their totem. She is one of them and their stories intertwine both as narrative and visual realities.

This creates an empathetic hologram that bridges the real concerns like a conduit with the fantastic, allowing the perception that justice in Hawkins will lead to justice in Ferguson, or on Wall Street, or any other place in the real world. They are connected by a powerful, supernatural talisman that has opened a door between two worlds.

Season Two vividly demonstrates this empathetic hologram as concern over Barb's disappearance increases and becomes a significant part of the season's story arc, culminating in a funeral and an acknowledgment of fault in her death by the Hawkins Laboratory and the United States Department of Energy. According to the Duffer Brothers, quoted in an article in *Vanity Fair*, #Justice-ForBarb had a direct impact on the plotting of Season Two. Matt Duffer stated that "People get very frustrated, under-standably, that the town doesn't seem to be really dealing with Barb" and that "what we want to do with hypothetical Season Two is to explore the repercussions of everything that happened." Hyperreal power thus becomes real power; it can affect change, unlike the use of the # in the real world for significant problems that are only rooted in our reality.

Adding to the hyperreal weirdness of it all, Shannon Purser received a nomination for Best Guest Actress in a Drama Series at the 2017 Emmy awards for her work on Season One of *Stranger Things*. This nomination was decried by many that follow and report on the television industry as less of an effort to honor an actor and more of an effort to create buzz for an already successful television product. It's clear that #JusticeForBarb played a key role in that decision, as guest starring roles are normally held by acclaimed actors who take a role on a television show to either boost its ratings or to add panache to a character that rarely appears. Purser's nomination was one of only three acting nominations that *Stranger Things* received at the 2017 Primetime Emmy Awards, with the other two going to two of the show's leads, David Harbour and Millie Bobby Brown. While #-focused social movements have a dubious track record of success when it comes to stopping real injustice, they've shown a solid capacity for use in marketing and promotion, which adds another complicated layer to the onion of meaning that hyperreality currently holds.

## The End

#JusticeForBarb shows us that real justice is fictional justice and vice-versa. Seeking #JusticeForBarb by inserting real life into the fictional world of Hawkins is a natural progression of the continually blending worlds of reality and fiction known as hyperreality. In this world, Demogorgons run free and the # has the ability to avenge the death of a forgotten young woman whose only sin is being bad at shotgunning beer. Now that Barb has been avenged, #JusticeForBarb is moot and the player characters who backed it will need a new quest. #JusticeForBob, anyone?

# 2
# Can Anything Good Come from the Upside Down?

ANDREW KUZMA

At the end of Season Two, our intrepid party and Steve (the ultimate babysitter) race to escape the Mind Flayer's tunnels only to be blocked by Dart. Dart (short for D'Artagnan) is a demodog, a young Demogorgon. Just one of these creatures was enough to terrorize the town of Hawkins in Season One. Now we've seen packs of them devour scores of people. So we fully expect Dart to attack the party. He's a monster from the Upside Down: of course he will attack! But he doesn't.

Dustin adopted Dart at the beginning of Season Two. He wasn't a Demodog then, just a slug—a little pollywog. After discovering Dart in the trash, Dustin deposits him in an aquarium and feeds him Three Musketeers. This was, perhaps, not the smartest decision. Despite living in a world in which Demogorgons exist, Dustin without hesitation brings a mystery animal into his bedroom. He would probably respond that he is on a curiosity voyage (and pollywog Dart is pretty cute). Besides, the two have a connection: they both love nougat. Even when Dustin finally realizes that Dart comes from the Upside Down, he defends his pet, insisting that even if Dart is from the Upside Down, "it doesn't automatically mean that he's bad."

"That's like saying just because someone's from the Death Star doesn't make them bad," Mike retorts. Mike has a point: the Upside Down is clearly evil. It is the Empire to Hawkins's Rebel Alliance, the Mordor to Hawkins's free peoples of Middle earth. Whatever affection Dustin might have for his unusual pet, we know that Dart is bad news. He eats Mews! Mike is right. Dart must be evil and given the opportunity would tear any one of them to pieces.

Except when given just that opportunity in the tunnels, Dart doesn't attack. Instead, he approaches Dustin cooing like a plaintive puppy. They have a moment: Dustin gives him a Three Musketeers and Dart lets them pass. The Demodog even has a forlorn look on his face as Dustin says goodbye. (Granted, it's a little difficult to read expressions on Dart's petal face). So Dart is from the Upside Down and a Demogorgon, but he still does something good. Maybe Dustin is right. Coming from the Upside Down doesn't automatically make you evil.

But how can you come from the Upside Down and still be good? If the Upside Down is evil—Death Star level evil—then we would expect everything from it to also be evil. The Upside Down looks pretty evil and it does some nasty things to Hawkins. What does it mean that Dart does something good? Maybe he didn't actually do something good; maybe he is just loyal to nougat. Or maybe Demogorgons aren't all bad.

## The Two Hawkinses

The Upside Down is cold, dark, damp, and rotten. Everything is cast in a sickly blue light. Spores flit about in the air and vines creep over everything. Nothing lives in the Upside Down (so far as we know) except the Mind Flayer, the Demogorgons and the vines (if they are "alive"). The party, with the help of their D&D manual, describe it as the Vale of Shadows:

> A dimension that is a dark reflection or echo of our world. It is a place of decay and death. A plane out of phase. A place of monsters. It is right next to you and you don't even see it.

The Upside Down is a mystery. It might be a parallel universe, an evil reality, or a possible future. Everyone has a theory.

What we can definitively say is that it has the same geography and the same structures as Hawkins. The Byers's home, the Harrington's pool, the library, the middle school, and even the ramshackle Castle Byers all exist in the Upside Down. For all intents and purposes, the Upside Down is Hawkins—just a different version of it. *Stranger Things* is about the conflict between these two Hawkinses.

Augustine of Hippo (354–430 C.E.), similarly, describes all of human history as a conflict between two cities: the city of God and the earthly city. Augustine was a Christian theologian and philosopher at a time when Christianity had just become the dominant religion of the Roman Empire. Rome was not what it once was and many pagans blamed Christianity for its decline (and especially for the sack of the city in 410 C.E.). Augustine wrote *The City of God*, in part, to defend the new religion. He argues that despite the enormous variety of cultures and governments, there are really just two types of human society: those who live according to the love of self and those who live according to the love of God. The former constitute the earthly city, the latter constitute the city of God. The city of God is oriented to good, while the earthly city is oriented to evil.

Both cities have existed throughout human history. Augustine uses Babylon and Jerusalem (as well as Rome and the Church) to symbolize them, but he also cautions his readers against identifying the cities too closely with specific institutions. Ideally the Church should be the city of God and Rome (the evil empire) should be the earthly city, but practically that is not always the case.

Augustine was realistic. He knew that people are not always what they appear to be. The Christian sitting in church might really belong in the earthly city, while the Roman outside might really belong in the city of God. Both cities actually exist—every human being is a member of one or the other—but we can never be sure to which city anyone belongs. History is rife with intimate betrayals: spouses turn on spouses, siblings on siblings, children on parents. We never actually know what's in another person's heart—even the hearts of those closest to us—so how can we presume to label whole populations as "good" or "evil"?

There is, in other words, no way to draw a border separating the cities. They are mixed together in the same time and space. What makes them different is not *where they are*, but *how their members interact*. The two cities are not different places; they are different moral orientations. And like the two cities, the main difference between the two Hawkinses is not one of location.

We don't really need to quibble about whether the Upside Down is a mirror universe, the dark side of our universe, or something else entirely. The two interact as if they exist in the same time and place. There are two Hawkinses, but there is only one world. We should be careful then, as Augustine warned, not to presume that we know who belongs in the Upside Down and who belongs in the "right side up."

## A Place of Decay and Death

Where is Will? It's the question on the lips of every character for the first few episodes of *Stranger Things*. The answer leads to quite a bit of confusion. When Mike, Dustin, and Lucas ask Eleven to take them to Will, she leads them to the Byerses' house. They don't find him. But Eleven is right: Will is there. They just can't see him because he's in the Upside Down. She's eventually able to explain "where" Will is by flipping their D&D board upside down. The two Hawkinses exist on the same board. Whether you are in the Upside Down or the right side up, you are always in the same place because it's the same board.

Characters can communicate between the two Hawkinses because they are actually in the same place. Will can talk to Joyce through the web of Christmas lights she weaves throughout the house, but only because he is in the Upside Down version of their house. (When Hopper and Joyce later visit the Upside Down, we discover that moving around in the Upside Down affects electricity in the right side up). At one point, Will even speaks to Joyce directly. It sounds like he's inside the walls, but when she peels back the wallpaper she sees him as if through a window (or better yet, a mirror). When she asks where he is, he replies: "It's like home, but it's so dark. It's so dark and empty. And it's cold." Will is home; he's just also in the Upside Down.

When Will flashes between the two Hawkinses, it's not *where* he is that changes; it's *how* he sees the world that shifts. He is always in the same place, whether it be his bathroom or the middle school. The two Hawkinses are (almost) exactly alike. The Upside Down version of the Byerses' bathroom even has the same soap dispenser as the "real" version. The only difference is that in the Upside Down everything is dark, empty, and covered in vines. At the end of Season Two, when the Mind Flayer peers down at the middle school, we can see that even the decorations for the Snow Ball are in the Upside Down. Either a committee of Demogorgons is setting up middle school dances, or the Upside Down is in the same world as the "real" Hawkins.

The unnerving implication is that both Hawkinses are "real." They are both part of the same world (or the same board). Indeed, Joyce's Christmas-light alphabet depends entirely on Will being able to see the letters that she has painted. The Upside Down is not a different world; it's a *different way of being* in this world. If we think of the two Hawkins as moral orientations (like Augustine's two cities), then we can explain how Dart can come from an evil place and still be good.

The fact that the two cities are often indistinguishable can help us to make sense of Dart's paradoxical goodness. The two cities are different because they have different orientations. Members of the city of God live according to the love of God. They act primarily not for their own benefit, but for the benefit of others. Members of the earthly city, on the other hand, live according to the love of self. They are ruled, Augustine explains, by *libido dominandi*, "the lust for domination." But just because they are different, doesn't mean they look different. They actually have a lot in common.

Compare, for example, the different parenting styles of Chief Hopper and Dr. Brenner. Hopper is not a perfect parent to Eleven. He is frequently overbearing, unreliable, and volatile. Despite his many flaws, however, Hopper's primary goal is to protect Eleven and to give her as normal a childhood as possible. Dr. Brenner, on the other hand, only ever seeks to dominate Eleven. He manipulates her so that he may achieve his own ends.

Hopper and Dr. Brenner occupy the same paternal role—they often "look" the same—but they have different moral orientations. Hopper's selfless concern for Eleven ultimately leads them to a more harmonious father-daughter relationship whereas Dr. Brenner's selfish attempt to use Eleven eventually leads to her running away from the lab. Different orientations lead to different results. The same holds true for the two cities. Augustine says that the city of God is bound for eternal life and peace with God, while the earthly city is doomed to eternal conflict and destruction, which he describes as an everlasting death.

The earthly city is "evil," but for Augustine that just means that it is broken. Evil is the absence of good, not the opposite of good. The opposite of good would be nonexistence. A nougat-less Three Musketeers is not the opposite of a Three Musketeers; it's just a terrible Three Musketeers. "Evil" things are corrupt versions of good things, which means that something about them is still good. After all, they must contain some goodness or there would be nothing to be corrupted. This understanding of evil also explains why the two cities can sometimes look the same.

The earthly city is what the city of God would look like without God. Not everything about it is evil, but it's missing something crucial. It's a Three Musketeers without the nougat. The chocolate shell is good, but without the nougat it's bound to disappoint. Augustine famously pointed to the temporal peace and the network of roads in the Roman Empire as good things provided by the earthly city. Rome was still the earthly city, but since the earthly city is not entirely evil, it was still able to produce these good results.

Similarly, at the end of the first season the Demogorgon "saves" the party by attacking the people from Hawkins Lab who are chasing them. The Demogorgon was not trying to help (in fact, it tries to eat them next). But even unintentionally saving them shows that the Party and the Demogorgon can have a common enemy (Hawkins Lab) and, consequently, that what is good for one can be good for both (no more Hawkins Lab).

The Upside Down, consequently, is not the opposite of the right side up. If it were, then it would be impossible for the two Hawkinses to share any common goods. The Upside Down is more like a broken or diseased version of Hawkins, Hawkins ruled by *libido dominandi*. The Mind Flayer, which seems to be the guiding force of the Upside Down, embodies this lust for domination. From its possession of Will to its invasion of Hawkins, the Mind Flayer seeks only to conquer and enslave. Moreover, this invasion has the effect of turning Hawkins into the Upside Down: the tunnels cause rot wherever they spread and each one possesses the same spore-filled atmosphere as the Upside Down. Like the earthly city, the Upside Down seeks to dominate and is bound for death and decay. But, also like the earthly city, it is not totally evil.

## Not Automatically Bad

It's not surprising that Mike would connect the Upside Down with the Death Star. Good and evil seem to be pretty clearly defined in Hawkins. If you suddenly find yourself surrounded by floating spores and creeping vines, then there's a good chance you've wandered into the Upside Down.

The simplicity of this dichotomy is attractive: if you're from the right side up, you're good, if you're from the Upside Down, you're evil. Augustine understood the temptation. We all want to draw clear boundaries. The Upside Down is the Hawkins guided by a lust for domination and destined for death and decay. The problem, as we have seen, is that the two Hawkinses are mixed together in this world. Augustine warns that those who look like enemies of the city of God might be destined to become citizens, while those who look like its citizens might actually be its enemies. We often don't know who is an enemy and who is an ally. We must ask: is this person (or monster) guided by a selfish love or a selfless love?

Dr. Brenner, as a human being, should belong in the right side up, but his actions suggest otherwise. He stole Eleven and Kali (Eight) from their families along with at least nine other children. For years he manipulated and abused Eleven, calling himself her "Papa" but only showing her affection as a reward. For example, when she disobeys him—by refusing to kill a cat—he abandons her to solitary confinement. In a fit of panic and terror, she kills the men carrying her to her cell. Only then, after coolly stepping over their dead bodies, does Dr. Brenner embrace her. He has no compassion for Eleven. All of his actions come from a selfish desire to control. Dr. Brenner is more frightening than the Demogorgon. Sure, the Demogorgon can smell blood and can drop unexpectedly into your living room. Really, though, it only behaves like a wild animal. Dr. Brenner chooses to act the way he does. The only other character in *Stranger Things* to demonstrate such a ruthless lust for domination is the Mind Flayer. "Papa" belongs in the Upside Down.

We might be tempted to say that all of Hawkins Lab belongs in the Upside Down too. Most of the nameless characters working there were willing to kidnap, torture, and kill. Dr. Brenner is not singularly evil, he's just part of an evil institution. Again, Augustine would warn us not to label institutions too quickly. Dr. Owens, Dr. Brenner's successor, turns out to be an ally of the right side up. We expect him to be another villainous scientist. He works diligently to cover up the work of Hawkins Lab and he not so subtly threatens Hopper, Jonathan, and Nancy. To top it all off, Paul Reiser, who portrays Dr. Owens, also played a very similar slimy bureaucrat in the 1986 classic, *Aliens* (a huge influence on *Stranger Things*). And yet, Dr. Owens refuses to burn the tunnels if it means killing Will, he risks his life to help guide Hopper, Joyce, and Bob to safety, and he fabricates a birth certificate for Eleven so that she can remain with Hopper. The lesson is clear: just because you're from Hawkins Lab, doesn't mean you're automatically bad.

All of which brings us back to Dart. Can a Demodog from the Upside Down be good? Since the Upside Down is not totally evil, we can't assume that its inhabitants are evil. After all, it's not even a different world, just a different way of being in this one. Dustin was right: just because you're from the Upside Down doesn't mean you're automatically bad. Augustine would agree that something that looks like an enemy from the earthly city could turn out to be an ally and vice versa. Dr. Brenner comes from the right side up, but he really belongs in the Upside Down. Dart is from the Upside Down, but he could belong in the right side up. It's not *where you are from* that matters, it's *how you act*.

What do Dart's actions tell us? Yes, he eats Mews. But Mews probably ate dozens of mice in his day. Dart is an animal too. More importantly, he lets Dustin, Mike, Lucas, Max, and Steve escape. Yes, Dustin distracts him with a Three Musketeers. That ploy only works, though, because Dart knows Dustin. Given his trill as he steps toward Dustin and the way he looks back at him as he leaves, we could even go so far as to say that Dart loves Dustin. It's not just the nougat; he lets them pass because he loves Dustin. If he had been given the chance, he might have turned out to be a good "dog."

Admit it, didn't you cry just a little bit at the final shot of Dart's lifeless body surrounded by candy wrappers? He may have been a petal faced monster from a dimension of darkness and death, but that doesn't make him automatically evil. Demogorgons aren't all bad.

# 3
# Save the Demogorgons!

Mikko M. Puumala

Can you imagine the angry townsfolk of Hawkins gathered outside Hawkins laboratory compound, waving signs and yelling "Save the Demogorgons! Free the Mind Flayer! Protect the Upside Down!"? Angry and worried people, trying to protect the *same* creatures that threaten our families, kidnap our children, and even eat our cats.

Most will find this just as unlikely as people waving "Save polio!" signs outside the World Health Organization headquarters. But how far out is the idea that morally, someone really ought to raise their voice for the weirdly cute (but slimy) baby demodogs, or even the cunning and deadly Demogorgon? And conversely, what right do we have to wipe them out?

Environmental philosophers deal with these kinds of nasty questions. They are nasty because many consistent answers to them lead us to unappealing and worrying conclusions about the morality of our common practices, like animal farming and nature conservation, or about our relation to dangerous predators. Even worse, answering such questions sheds light to our own place in the great scheme of things, and in that light, we don't always look so good. It might be the case that we are no better than the Mind Flayer, or no less dangerous and invasive than the Demogorgon.

Since the dawn of our species, we have slain the large beasts roaming in the vicinity of our encampments, which has, to the great regret of later generations, caused species to go extinct and even the destruction of complete ecosystems. Given that our current biological and ecological understanding being better; our destructive force greater than ever; and our circle of morality expanding in a quickening pace, stopping to ask these questions is more important than ever before. Especially now that a portal to another dimension—a whole new mysterious ecosystem with unknown species—has opened in the small Midwestern town of Hawkins.

## The Moral Considerability of Demogorgons

Discriminating against a living being on the basis of its species is *speciesism*. The term was coined by Richard Ryder in 1970 and made famous by Peter Singer in his book *Animal Liberation*. Species is basically the same for speciesism as race is for racism or sex is for sexism: an arbitrary biological fact about someone or something that is taken as a reason for different treatment without any further justification.

Not allowing Dustin's pet monster Dart to apply for a driver's license when he reaches maturity is *not* speciesist because we can come up with a justification for such discrimination, like Dart's lacking an ability to understand traffic rules. Putting Dart into a washing machine out of curiosity would be speciesist, especially if Dustin believed that it doesn't matter what we do to non-humans for fun. Or, it would be speciesist for Dustin to adopt Dart as a pet, but only feed his cat Mews and let Dart starve because it is not a member of a typical household animal species. Actually, feeding Dart a little *more* could've eventually saved poor Mews' life, as she was in fact eaten by the little rascal in "Will the Wise." So maybe there is a moral in the story along these lines, after all: Kids, don't neglect the needs of a living thing based on its species!

But are we being speciesist towards ants and grass when we prefer building a house instead of respecting their peaceful existence? A line must be drawn here. When drawing such lines, the environmental philosopher is discussing *moral considerability*, which directly sets the boundaries for our moral considerations. A being that we must take into account in our moral decisions is morally considerable. We can determine which kinds of creatures are morally considerable by seeing how well they match some criteria for moral considerability.

We should start from somewhere easy. Humans must be morally considerable (worthy of moral consideration) or else discussion of morality wouldn't make any sense. But what is it that makes Joyce morally considerable but not other living things, like the ones killed for the comfort food casserole Karen made for Joyce in "Holly, Jolly"?

Among philosophers, one of the leading candidates would probably be *intelligence*. Humans are different from the Demogorgon by intelligence, and if intelligence is a morally relevant criteria for moral considerability, then we can treat the Demogorgon differently from humans (without being speciesists). Demogorgons don't seem to form societies, play Dungeons & Dragons, invent walkie-talkies, or philosophize.

In *The Descent of Man*, Charles Darwin noted that human intelligence differs from other mammals not by kind, but by degree (p. 105). We are not *unique* because of our intelligence, although many of us are in many respects far more intelligent than other animals. So rather than intelligence per se, it is *high intelligence* that must be the relevant criterion.

But think about the Demogorgon preying on the scientist running for his life in "The Vanishing of Will Byers." Think about how cleverly it sits and waits in the elevator for the prey to arrive right where it wanted him to. The origin of our intelligence is sometimes (probably with some error) associated with the hunter-gatherers hunting for large mammals in groups. Who would you bet on, team *H for Humans* or team *D for Demogorgons* in catching a mammoth? Exactly. Demogorgons don't necessarily vote in the elections, play music with synthesizers, or nostalgize with past decade cultural artifacts, but they do outperform us in cunning, instinct, and team playing.

## The Moral Importance of Dart's Pain

It has turned out awkwardly difficult to provide a satisfactory criterion for moral considerability that would limit our moral considerations *only to humans* and *all humans* at the same time. High intelligence is a poor candidate for other obvious reasons as well. Adult pigs are far more intelligent than human babies, but you wouldn't consider eating a baby instead of a pig, right? Furthermore, we want to include comatose patients and toddlers in our moral considerations as well. Consequently, we might be interested in opening up our moral boundaries a little bit.

A much more inclusive criterion for moral considerability is *sentience*. By sentience we mean being able to suffer and feel pleasure. As Jeremy Bentham, the grand-daddy of utilitarianism, famously put it, "The question is not, Can they *reason?* nor, Can they *talk?* but, Can they *suffer?*" (*Introduction*, Chapter 17, Section 1). According to Peter Singer, sentience is a requirement for having interests in the first place (*Animal Liberation*, pp. 7–8). Thus, only sentient creatures are the ones that fit into our moral considerations. Sentientism is a moral doctrine which holds that all sentient creatures are morally considerable.

However, sentientism is not a perfectly clear-cut doctrine. We can be pretty certain that chimpanzees are sentient in the relevant sense, but not so sure about ants and sea cucumbers. How about the other-dimensional creepy crawlies from the Upside Down? Dustin took pretty good care of Dart, but the ungrateful pollywog went and ate Meows. Not much affection there. But the little one was still receiving food from Dustin, which suggests that it is capable of receiving nurture from a parent. Does this mean that the Demogorgons in general take care of their cubs? Perhaps. But more importantly, we saw that Dart was sensitive to heat and light. When the kids examined it and Mike turned a lamp over it, Dart reacted as if it was in pain ("The Pollywog"). For sentientism, pain is enough!

## Is the Mind Flayer a Moral Agent?

If what the kids read from the Dungeons & Dragons monster manual is true, and the Mind Flayer is a good metaphor ("analogy!") for the Shadow Monster, then there might be a good reason to hold the Mind Flayer as something more than just a morally considerable being we must take into account in our actions. Is it a moral agent, and an evil one, at that? Is it responsible for its actions?

Evil must be stopped, and you don't need a monster manual to figure that out. In "The Mind Flayer" Dustin says that the Mind Flayer thinks of itself as a master race, and its aim is to conquer the inferior races, including humans.

STEVE: Like the Germans?

DUSTIN: Uh, the Nazis?

STEVE: Yeah, yeah, yeah, the Nazis.

DUSTIN: If the Nazis were from another dimension, totally. ("The Mind Flayer")

This leaves open the questions about Demogorgons and the plant life of the Upside Down, but at least stopping the Mind Flayer would be perfectly fine if it truly is an evil creature that can make plans (like the trap it used Will to set) and desire things (like, well, taking over our world).

However, this kind of responsibility (and moral agency) requires a level of awareness that we can't be sure the Mind Flayer has. Just as we can't hold a spider responsible for laying a trap to a fly, we are probably not able to hold the Mind Flayer responsible for laying traps for people.

## Keystone Species in the Upside Down

There might actually be good reasons to *protect* the Demogorgons or even the Mind Flayer. Sometimes positive discrimination is called for. This means favoring previously discriminated or disadvantaged groups. In this case, we might give extra resources and special treatment to the members of some species that are nearly extinct. The living conditions for pandas resemble all-inclusive hotels if you compare them to where some farm animals live. Is it speciesist? If not, it is probably because pandas are *rare* and extra effort is needed to keep them around. Rarity, then, would be a justified reason for positive discrimination.

The Mind Flayer seems to be pretty rare. So are the Demogorgons. We have seen only a dozen Demogorgons and one Mind Flayer. Perhaps they are extremely endangered!

Cracking an opening to another dimension already risked them, but fortunately the life in the Upside Down seems pretty resilient in the face of outside influence. The scientists tried burning the vines ("Dig Dug") and multiple shots have been fired against its inhabitants without any effect ("The Upside Down," "The Lost Sister"). Even the diet of demodogs and demogorgons is very diverse, as they devoured humans, deer, cats, and slices of ham.

Also, the Upside Down adds a whole new biome to the known biodiversity, which is typically a good thing. The more biodiversity, the better. We don't even have to assume that all sentient beings have equal moral value since biodiversity can add to the overall good of humankind. It is possible to justify environmentalist ideas based on human wellbeing, or even on the thought that only humans have moral standing. This line of thinking is called *anthropocentrism*. For example, destroying the Amazon is sometimes objected on the grounds that there might be unknown sources for medicine yet to be found. Who knows what we might find in the Upside Down?

From what we know, the Mind Flayer is a key player in the Upside Down. When we first saw it, it seemed like a creature of its own, distinct from the Demogorgons and the plant-like life in the Upside Down. It looked like a giant spider looming on the horizon ("Trick or Treat, Freak"). However, in "The Mind Flayer" the kids describe it as hivemind or a superorganism. Every other living thing in the Upside Down is somehow connected to it. When a vine from the Upside Down is burned, Will feels the pain because the Mind Flayer has him in its control ("The Spy"). All of this suggests that hurting the Mind Flayer itself hurts a lot of living organisms in the ecosystem of the Upside Down.

The Mind Flayer might even be what ecologists call a *keystone species*—take that down and many other species in the ecosystem will perish. In this sense, it might have been extremely dangerous for Eleven to use her powers against the Mind Flayer in "The Gate." It could've died, taking down all the vine-like plant life and Demogorgons with it. In terms of nature conservation, the science team member torching the Upside Down plant life near the gate was a little bit over the top, too.

On the other hand, speciesism goes both ways, fortunately. Just because the biological life in Upside Down is *new* to us doesn't mean we can favor it over the well-known and boring life in our own dusty old dimension. There doesn't have to be anything inherently wrong in making changes to nature. Sometimes one species replaces another. But even if life in our dimension and in the Upside Down would be equally valuable, there would've been *less biodiversity* had the Upside Down spread to our dimension. The thing with the Upside Down is that life from it spreads aggressively, and it seems to kill more life than it brings.

As we saw in "Trick or Treat, Freak", all the poor pumpkins in the fields and even the trees in the nearby forest were infected by the life spreading underground through the tunnels. Beneath the fields, in the tunnels, there were spores poisonous to breathe ("Dig Dug"). If the Upside Down used to be a dimension almost identical to ours, it evidently suffered from heavy biodiversity loss, and our dimension was going to be next.

Who knows how bad things would've gotten if Eleven hadn't shut the gate, even though it required risking the Mind Flayer's well-being at the same time? In that elevator beneath the laboratory, Eleven used her telekinetic powers to close the gate and fend off the Mind Flayer ("The Gate"). In doing so, she prevented major losses of life and diversity. So, in this sense, the conservationists should be happy for what Eleven and the others did.

## The Wicked Who Dull the Land

So, was it good that the Mind Flayer was stopped? At least it averted another pick-your-pumpkin catastrophe and a ruined Halloween, but also potential losses in biodiversity and unnecessary suffering of local sentient beings. If these things count as morally important, then in this sense it was good.

Yet, this has an inconvenient moral side-effect to it. Imagine that the Mind Flayer would've gotten its way and started inhabiting our dimension, spreading its favored biological system and breeding demogorgons to finally take over the Earth. First the US Midwest would've fallen, then the whole nation, until the rest of the continent was under the control of that evil creature.

Perhaps more humans would've been put under its spell as Will was, doing the Mind Flayer's, well, *will*. Our behavior would've changed like Will's did. Will clearly isn't a liar, but the Mind Flayer made him lie to the science team to set up a trap ("The Spy"). Our kind would've turned into cattle, our rich emotional lives suppressed under the control of a new master, to serve its purposes. The Earth's diverse nature would've perished into dull monocultures, only trees and grass still standing.

And now, ask yourself, how is the actual world very much different from the Upside Down? Isn't our dimension already ruled by one species, while other animals are enslaved and nature's diversity diminishes? How is the Mind Flayer any worse than we are? Just like the same, dull vines and spores all over the Upside Down, we can't escape the grasp of human influence in our world. Have you ever seen a big city from an airplane? They seem to crawl endlessly on the land-scape, devouring everything in their way.

If it was good that Eleven shut the gate and expelled the Mind Flayer, then it would also be good if she was able to somehow shut *humans* out of this dimension and stop us from turning the world into something quite similar to the Upside Down. This is an uneasy thought. There must be a difference between us and the Mind Flayer. One candidate for that might be simply origin: we originate from here, whereas the Mind Flayer is an invader.

## Uprooting the Upside Down

We can easily imagine a poster on the bulletin board of Hawkins Middle School pleading for students to volunteer in weeding out some invasive plant species in Mirkwood. Is it speciesist to discriminate a species based on its origin? If it was, a bulk of conservationist agenda would be morally du-bious, and we don't want that. Invasive species are evaluated based on their harmfulness to the local ecosystem. They must go so that something original can survive. It is also a matter of leveling out the score: invasive species often lack any natural enemies in the new ecosystem, so they take over while the local species don't stand a chance. The spreading of the Upside Down fits this definition pretty well.

The conservationist justification goes somewhat like this: It is not only morally permissible, but morally praiseworthy to kill harmful invasive species, because they cause such harm to the defenseless local flora and fauna. Eleven giving hell to the Mind Flayer can have a conservationist justification because it eventually protected the local ecosystem from outside threats. The boys shooting the Demogorgon with a wrist-rocket was justified because we ought to get rid of such invaders, as was the military police opening fire against the monster in Hawkins Middle School.

This is all assuming, of course, that we were here first.

If killing invasive species is either morally permissible or even praiseworthy, then Eleven and the other kids did nothing wrong, or were even doing something good. The environmentalists wouldn't have any grounds for their pro-demogorgon demonstrations in front of Hawkins lab. Instead, they should wear "Eleven" T-shirts to honor her conservationist struggle for the whole biological community of Hawkins, Indiana.

## Because Its Face Opened Up and It Ate My Cat

Before praising Eleven's environmental heroism, the environmental philosopher is puzzled by two questions. First of all, what counts as an invasive species? Second, does it really provide a sufficient reason to allow killing? Invasive species are non-native, as they come from somewhere else. Although both are non-native, exotic species are not invasive, since they don't cause harm to the local ecosystem. The harmfulness of invasive species is a morally relevant factor that makes it also praiseworthy to get rid of them, although it would probably not be the case with exotic species. However, just being aggressive towards and harmful to the local ecosystem is not a sufficient condition for a species to be invasive, as we have many native species that act destructively. If a native species gets an advantage and wipes out other native species from the ecosystem, it is still not invasive.

So, in what sense are demogorgons invasive? They are exotic, that's for sure, and harmful is an understatement (ask poor Barb Holland who got snatched near Steve Harrington's swimming pool in "The Weirdo on Maple Street"). They are *deadly*. But to count as invasive a species has to be non-native, that is, from some other ecosystem. And this is where it gets tricky.

First of all, the two dimensions are causally connected. Will is able to communicate to his mother through the Christmas lights, and evidently hears her speaking, since he can answer consistently to her questions. In "Holly, Jolly," Joyce asks Will "Where are you?" and Will replies "R-I-G-H-T H-E-RE" through the lights and the letters painted on the ceiling. Also, Eleven is able to receive and play Will singing The Clash's "Should I Stay or Should I Go" through the walkie talkie. If the two dimensions are causally connected, it is not clear that demogorgons are non-native.

Also, in the Upside Down most things are hauntingly familiar to our world. The buildings, trees, and furniture are the same, but covered with creepy slimy vines of some kind. Remember when Joyce hears Will banging the ceiling and she desperately tears down the wallpaper to be able to see him? Will says "It's like home but it's so dark, so dark, and so empty!"

And now that the connection between our two worlds is open, the demogorgons are able to come through the walls and prey on their targets interdimensionally. Is it far-fetched that if they have memories, they have memories of the *same* Castle Byers that Joyce has when she reminisces about the time before Will went missing? Or that the hole in the base of the tree they use for entering and exiting (sort of) is the very *same* tree, but perhaps just a different aspect of it? In what way would the demogorgons be non-native? Is it important that they came from the *same* environment of a parallel dimension?

## Who's the Invader?

Still, it's not certain that demogorgons *originate* from the environment parallel to ours. As Mr. Clarke explains to the children about the mechanisms of interdimensional traveling in "The Flea and the Acrobat," we're like an acrobat on a string, able to stand on top of it and move back and forth. A flea is able to do the same, but also walk along or even below the string. So perhaps the demogorgons originate from somewhere that is kind of between dimensions and are able to move from one dimension to the other. Another plausible explanation is that they work like the plagues of locusts devastating crops. When one dimension is completely exploited, they move on to the next.

Mr. Clarke said that it would require huge amounts of energy to crack open a gate between dimensions, which happened when Eleven interacted with a demogorgon for the first time. She used her mental abilities to reach out to the creature, panicked, and the force of her emotions was so strong that it tore a hole in whatever holds our two dimensions separate.

Was there another Eleven in the pre–Upside Down version of the dimension parallel to ours who cracked an opening to some other dimension, from where the Mind Flayer and the demogorgons breached into that dimension, now known as the Upside Down? Are we in a regressive loop? Has this cycle gone on for ages? Did Eleven not catch up with Hopper and the others in that dimension, which prevented her from shutting down the gate before it was too late? We may never know, but perhaps it's enough to say that we can't be certain about the non-nativeness of demogorgons, and the fact that they are harmful to the ecosystems they come in contact with is enough to grant permission to get rid of them.

Yet, the fact that a species is invasive should not mean that we can do just whatever we want to them. Whether a species is invasive or not, there must be some limits to what we can do to them or how much we can kill them off. For the second question, if being invasive is sufficient for the permissibility of killing a creature, what would stop us from killing humans, too? If we want to avoid speciesism, that is, discrimination on the basis of belonging to a certain species, we would at least need to show that there is some other morally relevant reason to let humans live but demogorgons die.

After all, the good folks of Hawkins, Indiana, are also an invasive species in America, as humans didn't evolve in that environment. They too lack natural enemies in there and are able to reproduce without competition. Further, humans cause the most environmental damage and unbalance in the local ecosystems. But it is not morally permissible to kill humans. Therefore, we could argue, without there being any morally relevant criterion for favoring humans instead of demogorgons, we shouldn't kill demogorgons (on those grounds). However, (supposedly) we *do* originate from this dimension, which gives us some edge.

Some have protested against killing invasive species on other grounds. The practice called *compassionate conservation* seeks ways to protect the native species without hurting the invaders. For example, in Australia vast numbers of non-native wildlife, such as cats and red foxes, are massacred with traps or 1080 poison, which causes a very painful death. Yet, those animals are there *because* of humans. And demogorgons are here *because* of humans. Demogorgons attacking us seems to be perfectly normal predatory behavior and letting the monsters in was our own fault. Clearly, they are not responsible for the deaths of Barb Holland and Bob Newby ("Remember, Bob Newby, Superhero"), but rather it was Dr. Brenner and his science team who enabled all these horrors. Eleven seemed to act in accordance with compassionate conservation by shutting down the portal to the Upside Down and preventing more unnecessary bloodshed.

## Kill the Bastard, Kill It Now!

So, according to anti-speciesism it is morally wrong to discriminate against a creature based on its species without a separate justification, and according to sentientism all sentient creatures are morally considerable and therefore it is wrong to hurt them. Demogorgons are sentient creatures, so killing them requires some special justification separate from the fact that they are not human. Them adding to the biodiversity is a morally relevant thing, but it loses its power since we can favor protecting our environment from them without being speciesists, as they are an invasive species to the whole of our dimension. And even the idea of compassionate conservation was more or less satisfied, as shutting them out from our dimension happened without too much unnecessary violence.

But while the demogorgons were still here, what justification did our heroes have in hurting them? Obviously, self-defense is morally permissible, so Jim Hopper did nothing wrong when he shot the demodogs ("Demogorgon, dogs. Demo-dogs. It's like a compound, it's like a play on words, you know") in the lobby of the lab ("The Mind Flayer"). But how far does self-defense go as an excuse to kill these beasts?

Protecting your loved ones and your community does seem to allow some activities that are otherwise morally not permitted. But this only covers the situations where demogorgons pose a direct threat. The fact that they are dangerous does not grant a general permission to kill them, or otherwise it would be morally okay to go and hunt down all the potentially dangerous animals like near-extinct tigers. Potential danger is not enough.

There is something worrying about the presence of dangerous creatures lurking in our vicinity. Tigers and wolves usually avoid human interaction. Sometimes a disturbed animal individual may have to be taken down if it comes too close, but other times we peacefully co-exist. On the other hand, no one is worried for the wellbeing of bacteria or viruses. There are no protests on behalf of smallpox, which continues its existence captive in super secure laboratories. Is the case of demogorgons more like tigers or small pox? Although demogorgons are dangerous in a way similar to tigers and wolves, they pose a constant threat to humans similar to diseases. Also, the toxic environment of the Upside Down and the evil schemes of the Mind Flayer are a constant threat. There is a conflict of interests in play.

## I'm Sorry. You Ate My Cat

From the very first moments of *Stranger Things*, it becomes painfully clear that the interests of humans and demogorgons are in conflict. Having a Demogorgon loose in your town would probably conflict with your interest to be safe, to be able to send you children to school knowing that they'll return in one piece (or at all), and so on. Does this conflict of interest prompt some non-speciesist justification for hunting the beast down?

Although we'd hold that all sentient beings have equal value, are equally morally considerable, or even have equal rights, there's bound to be some conflict of interests between them. In *The Case for Animal Rights* (1983), Tom Regan presents a thought experiment where four humans and one dog are stuck on a lifeboat about to sink under the weight of all of them combined. One of them has to be sacrificed so the others can survive. Which one? Regan holds that although they all have inherent value, the dog must go. The life of a human is still more precious, because our lives are more vivid and deep with different experiences compared to a dog (p. 285). If the people in Hawkins and the demogorgons can't all fit in, surely the demogorgons must go.

When I was teaching a course on environmental philosophy, one of my students wasn't very impressed with Regan's solution. She noted that the only sentient creature in that lifeboat who wasn't there by its own will was the dog. All the others took a risk knowingly when they boarded the ship. Therefore, one of the humans must go. Again, there is something artificial in nonhumans getting into these conflicts of interests, and there is indeed something worrying in letting them suffer the consequences.

It all boils down to the artificial nature of the demogorgons being here, the Mind Flayer getting ahold of our world, and the Upside Down spreading dangerously in tunnels underneath Hawkins. Artificial or not, it was accidental. No one intended to crack open a portal to another dimension. Even Dr. Brenner, megalomaniac that he is, probably didn't even dream of such possibilities.

Also, after the passage was opened between the dimensions, the evil in the Upside Down started spreading, as if it was waiting opportunistically for something like that to happen. Perhaps the lifeboat example should be modified a bit to be truly analogous: a lifeboat is in the open sea, with four people and a clever wolf on board, and it has become clear that the lifeboat can't hold all of them. Which one should go? The wolf is the only one presenting a constant danger to the others, apart from adding to the total weight of the passengers. But perhaps it was the human who accidentally left a lunchbox open and lured the wolf onto the boat. Can we blame the wolf for that?

## Friends of the Upside Down

The environmental philosopher asks a lot of questions, as we have seen. And some of them force us to further question our own actions. The old hero-villain thing where the hunter kills the wolf and saves the day is not so clear-cut anymore. If we opened up our morality just a little bit and extended it to involve other things than humans as well, then things both fascinating and scary may happen. This allows us to see the world from a whole new perspective, like a new dimension had opened up. And as we have seen, disturbing things crawl in when this is done.

But, for now, a satisfyingly happy ending has been reached. The gate to the Upside Down has been shut and further injustices and immoralities prevented. The crowd in front of Hawkins Laboratory may be relieved and disperse, while the organizing committee for animal justice retreats to their club house, getting ready to print a dozen "I'm with Eleven!" T-shirts to show their support on keeping the two biospheres separate, as they were, and as they probably should be.[1]

---

[1] This chapter was written with the support of Maj and Tor Nessling Foundation.

# II

## The Joy of the Creepy

# 4
# The Slimy, Macabre, and Horrific in *Stranger Things*

CLARA NISLEY

Horror series often depict terrifying and disgusting monsters and *Stranger Things* is no exception. From the first episode of Season One, we find ourselves engrossed by a gruesome, threatening monster that has been released from its dark, slimy world onto Hawkins, Indiana. As the audience, we love it—and *Stranger Things* has proved to be popular. But why do we take pleasure in the macabre, slimy, and horrific in *Stranger Things*?

## Why Are We Drawn to the Macabre and Horrific?

Our fascination with *Stranger Things* suggests that we have an unquenchable thirst for the macabre, slimy, and horrific. *Stranger Things* draws us into the horrific with scenes of an ominous and threatening nature and piques our curiosity with the appearance of a portal into another world. The sense of impurity and the feelings of disgust in response to its horrific monsters are the reasons that we're fascinated by them. Consider the Demogorgon. This iconic monster directly crosses the boundaries between worlds. It lives in the Upside Down—a place hostile to humans—yet the monster is able to easily cross into this world, falling outside what we know of as the natural order of things.

The philosopher Nöel Carroll suggests that part of why we take pleasure in such unnatural or frightening monsters is our curiosity about their origins and purposes. This curiosity is undoubtedly amplified by how unnatural, frightening, or disgusting the creatures are. In *Stranger Things*, the disclosure of the monster would not interest us nearly as much if it were *not* grotesque and horrific . . . our sense of distress and disgust concerning its dangerous and impure properties is required.

Even so, we're challenged with the question: how did the monster enter our world? We have a desire to learn about the monster's existence and its entrance into this world. *Stranger Things* piques our curiosity with the prospect of something that, in our world, would be unbelievable. The show renders the mysterious more accessible through the construction of a world where a small town bears witness to the monster in their midst. Nonetheless, watching *Stranger Things* requires speculation about what's really going on regarding events that we can't explain fully. We, as audience members, want to discover the heretofore impossible and unnatural for ourselves.

## Monsters in Shadow

The *Stranger Things* monster sends chills up our spines as it terrorizes Hawkins, Indiana. From its very first scene, it crosses into our world and enters Hawkins National Laboratory. It captures one of the scientists who tried to escape in an elevator. The scene is suspenseful, designed to provoke our curiosity and elicit a sense of horror. It cuts off, and we hear Mike say, "Something is coming. Something hungry for blood."

Now we watch as the boys Mike, Dustin, Lucas, and Will play Dungeons & Dragons. "What if it's the Demogorgon?" Dustin asks. It's the Demogorgon. Will tries to fireball the Demogorgon but fails. He rolls a seven, and his character was caught by the Demogorgon. As Will rides his bike, a shadowed alien creature appears in front of him and he loses control of his bike. He hears an eerie noise coming from the dark and runs into his house calling for his mom. He looks out the window and sees the monster coming toward the house. The monster has the power to unchain the door, so Will runs into the shed where he disappears. We haven't seen the monster yet, but it's our thoughts about the monster, our thoughts of the fearsome and disgusting monster involved in Will's disappearance, that frightens us. Carroll tells us that *monsters provoke disgust* and disgust is required for an audience to gain the pleasure involved an audience's becoming curious of the unknown.

The next day we watch as three scientists with biohazard suits go down the elevator where the scientist had disappeared from the previous night. As they walk through the hall full of spores in the air, they find an opening that appears to be a portal where the monster came through. While inside they find a tentacled and slimy breathing living entity, sprawled on a wall. We are reminded of the monster in its slimy dwelling. Our idea of the monster is that it's associated with gooey, slimy ooze—and contact with it might contaminate us.

In Episode 2 ("The Weirdo on Maple Street"), we watch as the scientists find a slimy goop oozing through the vent in the shed where Will went missing. Our reaction to the gleaming tentacled creature and its slimy goop mimics the scientists who avoid direct contact with the creature and its residue goop. Our assumption that the hazmat suits are to avoid contamination form the basis of our emotions of nausea and repugnance. These emotions do not require that we believe in the monster's existence for them, and particularly our disgust, to be very real. And our curiosity about the monster and its origins comes at a price, the cost being nausea and revulsion.

## Beware of Growling Noises

One night, while at Steve Harrington's pool party, a sulky Barb Holland sits alone on the diving board, contemplating her friendship with Nancy Wheeler, Mike's older sister. We watch as drops of blood splash onto the water, sinking and dispersing in the water. A second later, Barb looks back as she hears a growling noise coming from behind her. We get a glimpse of the monster, but we never see its face—the thought of Barb's peril alone frightens us.

This is what Carroll calls "art-horror." It's an emotion brought about by some physically felt agitation that has been caused by our evaluation of the situation. This is part of why we engage with the emotions of horror. Nancy's curiosity, her progress in exploration and discovery, and her prediction that something horrible has happened to Barb evoke in us a fear of the realization of the awful truth. Carroll describes how we experience these emotions physically—the revelation of the monster agitates and our hearts literally pound. Barb wakes up in the Upside Down gagging, her hair and clothes sodden with a rusted-colored goop. She screams for her friend Nancy. As the monster grabs her and pulls her back into the Upside Down, the sight of her horrified face upsets us (and maybe we scream too).

Our pleasure in seeing the monster as Barb wakes up is part of the appreciation for *Stranger Things*. It satisfies our curiosity of the monster's existence, as we continue to engage in the story by being involved in the process of discovery through Nancy's curiosity. Our response is based on our thoughts about the dangerousness and impurity of this inexplicable and putrid monster that lives in an alternate dimension. The monster is unwholesome, it is impure, it arises from an oozing environment imaginably from a contaminated biochemical waste. The very point is that such images of the grotesque, slimy, and horrific lures us, but Carroll suggests that it's our feelings of fear and disgust that form part of the fascination—and the confirmation of the monster's existence reinforces our desire to watch.

But Nancy has yet to discover its existence, and her detection of a creature lurking behind Barb—a photograph that Jonathan had taken while Barb was sitting on the diving board—entices Nancy to search for it. Carroll claims that the fundamental pleasure with respect to horror fiction is a matter of fascination with the categorically transgressive beings. A being that is interstitial—occupying spaces between the earthly and unearthly worlds—is prone to be found disturbing. The monster is a creature we cannot categorize. It defies comprehension. Is it merely an earthly creature (like a bear or lion) we don't yet know? The monster has not been manifested, so it is our imagination as to what this creature is that contributes to our curiosity.

In "The Flea and the Acrobat," Nancy and Jonathan search for the creature in the woods. She hears a noise, revealed to be a deer that appears to have been hit by a car. The deer is suffering, so she and Jonathan agree to kill it out of mercy. But before Jonathan could kill it, an unseen animal or monster drags it away. It's regarded as an impure crawling creature that is earthbound. But, when Nancy sees the creature's hideous face, after watching the monster feeding on the deer, we see that the creature is not earthly. Its low guttural sound does not belong to any animal that we can categorize belonging to this earth. As the audience of horror fictions, our emotions are supposed to parallel those of the human protagonists of the fictions. To say it slightly differently, we are supposed to share certain elements of these characters' feelings about unnatural monsters—these characters' fear, disgust, curiosity.

Our thoughts of the dangerous and impure properties of monsters thus explains our art-horror emotions. Nancy's physical threats from the monster; our thoughts of Barb as she tried to escape it in the Upside Down; our disgust from the slime and dirt associated with it explain how we're art-horrified. While we don't really believe that the monster exists, we relate to the characters, and their fear becomes our fear. Their disgust at the thought of these monstrous aberrations become our own disgust—and the legacy of these creatures in our memory stays with us.

## The Macabre

In Episode 5, we find the depiction of death horrifying. Devin reads to Mike and Lucas from the Dungeons & Dragons handbook about the Vale of Shadows. Devin explains that the Vale of Shadows is "a dimension that is a dark reflection, or echo, of our world. It is a place of decay and death, a plane out of phase, a place of monsters. It is right next to you and you do not even see it." It's an unearthly and horrifying place where Nancy followed the trail of blood from the wounded deer. It is a place of darkness, blood, and decay.

Nancy entered and was fortunate enough to escape the imprisonment and death by the creature's claws. We see the creature hunched over its kill, the aftermath of its deadly capabilities, indicating that the death of Barb could have been just as macabre. The very sight of the monster in its dwelling, eating the carcass is part of the delight we take in our enjoyment of the macabre.

We think of Leontius's story as related by Plato in *The Republic*, where Plato explains how we can feel both disgust and pleasure in looking at the corpse. In *Revealing Art,* Matthew Kieran reinforces Plato's point that we ironically delight in the grotesque. At some level we delight in Barb's corpse, with dark rimmed eyes, dark-blue lips, and a torn cheek where we can see her teeth. The macabre scene with Barb, devoid of life, lying in the putrid Upside Down covered in slime instill feelings of fear and debased pleasure. Thus, while Carroll highlights the importance of our disgust for our horror experience, Kieran also emphasizes that we may paradoxically "delight in what we (ought to) desire not to desire." The paradoxical nature of the macabre is exactly this feeling of dread alongside the pleasure of satisfying our curiosity through the disclosure of Barb's death and its circumstances.

## The Horrific

The horrific is the knowledge that the monster is threatening the children of Hawkins. We see that fear can be the foundation for encounters with the awe-inspiring monster. The frightened Nancy is not able to sleep alone. Eleven's fear, when she enters the monster's world, causes her terror and anxiety at the thought of confronting it. Yet Carroll states that once the monster is disclosed alongside its bestial taste for blood, the monster, generally, has to be confronted, and the narrative is driven by the question of whether the creature can be destroyed. However, even at this point the drama of ratiocination can continue as further discoveries—accompanied by arguments, explanations, and hypotheses—reveal features of the monster that will facilitate or impede the destruction of the creature.

In "The Upside Down" Nancy and Jonathan set the trap for the Demogorgon. We see the instance of this in Nancy's discussion with Jonathan. They're convinced that the monster can be enticed with blood. There hypothesis is that the creature, although otherworldly, can be understood naturalistically. Nancy's curiosity about its possibilities and the events that challenge the way she has categorized the world provoke her into catching the monster. Nancy and Jonathan buy a bear trap to catch it, as if the monster were an animal they can hunt. There is without a doubt a certain invitation hidden in fear—a certain macabre allure that motivates Nancy and Jonathan. Just like the characters in *Stranger Things*, we too are fascinated by the possibility of capturing the monster. Our interests, ideally, are satisfied by the possibility that it can be destroyed.

First they have to draw blood to attract the monster. We finally get a good look at the monster when it opens its petal-like mouth. Eventually, Nancy, Jonathan, and Steve lure and catch it in the bear trap and light it on fire. We believe the danger is over. But, when Jonathan puts out the flames, the monster is nowhere to be found. Here we see that our desire to discover how the monster can be killed is not fully satisfied. It defies our conception of nature as our heroes are unable to destroy it, even with fire. The monster exceeds in horribleness because of its supernatural and unearthly abilities. We continue to be curious about its impossibility. Yet, as Carroll argues, this is why we watch—we stare in awe as we try and comprehend that which should not be.

## The Slimy and Grotesque

Such a repulsive looking monster is utterly disturbing in appearance and is violently presented, eating a large egg covered in a slimy webbing. The imagination fails to comprehend what is presented. The unearthly creature and the unnatural appetite for the slime-covered egg produces a feeling of displeasure. Its feeding on the slimy egg gives rise to the paradoxical feelings of disgust and fascination.

We're grossed out by the unnatural, but we're fascinated as we watch the crude, barbaric creature with its physical features and the visual irregularities that arouse our attention. As we struggle to process these feelings and try to find harmony and order in the world, the displeasure brings to the mind a resulting paradoxical positive response.

If Noell Carroll is right, and I think he is, we feel an aversion, but it is simultaneously overcome by gazing in fascination at the transgressive qualities of the monster. In *The Pleasure of Tragedy*, Susan Feagin asserts that the *gross-out* specifically must be a part of our attraction in viewing the egg covered in a web of slime, just as Kieran proposes that our pleasure arises from the grotesque properties thereof. When we watch Will coughing up a slug-like creature with yellow-bluish skin that crawls down the drain, our disgust amplifies our enjoyment and fascination.

At some level, even if we wouldn't be honest with ourselves about it, we enjoy the revulsion. This enjoyment is amplified further as *Stranger Things* also routinely piques our curiosity, raising *just enough* questions about the unnatural creature to glue us to our seats for season after disgusting season.

# 5
# Horror Appeals to Our Dual Nature

FRANKLIN S. ALLAIRE AND KRISTA S. GEHRING

It seems like every other week there is a new comic, television show, or movie that features something dark and disgusting. The morbid and macabre have always held a special place in our hearts, evidenced by how armies of flesh-eating undead, blood-sucking vampires, pus-filled mutants, and killer clowns (from outer space?) have gained in popularity in recent years.

*Stranger Things* is a prime example of how tapping the well of horrific creatures, which has driven other monster-based television programs such as *The Walking Dead* and *The X-Files*, can lead to success.

Tales of horror and suspense seem always to have had a significant place in the narratives we tell to one another, as their roots can be traced to ancient origins in folklore and religious traditions. Stories of death, monsters, demons, and the afterlife are found in all cultures and tap into things that are difficult to understand about ourselves. Humans voraciously consume horror artifacts, whether they be fiction, movies, or television shows.

For example, 2018 was a very good year for horror at the box office. Moviegoers spent over $900 million to watch horror movies such as *A Quiet Place*, *Halloween*, and *The Nun*—the top three highest grossing horror movies that year—on the big screen. That same year, *Get Out* won an Academy Award for Best Original Screenplay. While *Stranger Things* may not technically be horror, it has many elements that are creepy, unsettling, and often horrific, and its success proves it has struck a nerve with many viewers.

In Noël Carroll's *The Philosophy of Horror*, he points out that most people have absolutely no *real* interest in coming into contact with the creepy, crawly, slimy, and disgusting things they love to watch on television and movies. There seems to be no limit to audiences' passion for zombie-related stories, yet how many zombie-loving individuals have any desire to visit an operating theatre, morgue, or funeral home?

As Carroll points out, we generally try to avoid things in the real world that disgust us (such as dead and decaying bodies, blood, rats, and insects), yet we are drawn to these very same things on both the large and small screens. To understand why our appetite for slimy and disgusting creatures and nightmarish situations is as insatiable as Eleven's for Eggos, we need to think about the things that we fear.

Like immersing ourselves in a sensory deprivation tank, our goal is to look beyond everyday corporeal fears (clowns, public speaking, snakes) and explore the existential fears and their philosophical connection to our human nature. Since we're not currently in danger of being overrun and hunted down by a pack of ravenous Demodogs, we have the luxury of pondering these fears and how they relate to our love of all things dark, disgusting, and horrific.

## What Are You Afraid Of?

Everyone's afraid of something. Small doses of fear help keep us safe, while more substantial amounts can be debilitating. Generally speaking, fear is a feeling stimulated by a perceived threat or danger. This perception causes changes in organ functions, metabolism, and ultimately guides our behavior (fight or flight). Many of our conscious fears are specific; for example, heights (*acrophobia*), flying (*aerophobia*), and germs (*mysophobia*) rank among the top fears among both adult men and women. However, physicist and cognition expert Dr. Karl Albrecht notes two fundamental fears—extinction and mutilation—that consciously and unconsciously guide our thinking and actions. The genius of *Stranger Things* has been the writers' and actors' abilities to trigger viewers' fears in multiple ways.

Extinction is often oversimplified as a "fear of death." While death can be pretty scary, the fear of extinction is more complicated. Albrecht explains that it's a fear of "annihilation, of ceasing to exist," which takes this fear out of the narrow idea of death and broadens it to the idea of *no longer being*. What if I just disappeared? What if my existence were somehow "erased"? Extinction  is so fundamental to our being that it guides everything from how we name our children to self-identifying with social groups to cross-cultural relations.

Mutilation refers to having our bodies invaded, injured, or maimed to the point where parts of our body don't function properly. This fear can also include feeling as if we're under attack or physically unsafe. Triggers for this fear are typically things like creepy-crawlies (spiders, insects, and snakes), animals you think would be dangerous to you (dogs, sharks, and scorpions), as well as perceived hazardous situations (crowds, germs, and needles).

The anxiety created by the fears of extinction and mutilation are particularly motivating, according to existentialist heavyweight Søren Kierkegaard, because humanity has a dual nature and experiences a tug-of-war between our *finitude*—the flesh and blood part of the self—and our *infinitude*—the abstract or heavenly part of the self.

The show's use of the "Demogorgon" throughout Season One plays into this notion of duality. The Demogorgon, in the fantasy role-playing game Dungeons & Dragons (D&D), is a powerful two-headed demon prince (also known by its much cooler name "the Lord of All that Swims in Darkness"). It's one of the more powerful creatures and villains in D&D whose figure Eleven uses when trying to explain the Upside Down and the creature that kidnapped Will. The Demogorgon's two heads, called Aameul (the left head) and Hethradiah (the right head), have individual minds and distinct personalities that both work together and seek to dominate and destroy each other.

Building on Kierkegaard's work, cultural anthropologist Ernest Becker explained that human beings have extremely powerful and creative brains capable of infinite creativity, but we are still housed in bodies that will eventually fail us, die, and decay. In *The Denial of Death* (2007) Becker describes humanity as standing apart from nature with an unusual dignity within the animal kingdom, yet hopelessly part of it.

Like D&D players, we have access to a variety of armor and shield types to buffer us against anxiety caused by reminders of our mortality and finitude. While D&D armor ranges from leather to chain mail to plate armor, our armor is social, cultural, and symbolic. However, like any armor, there are strengths and weaknesses. Our most basic armor protects us against the gross, disturbing, disgusting and possibly dangerous things that trigger our everyday fears. Social, cultural, and symbolic armor, everything from flags to religion, to local sports teams, is used to protect us from existential threats. This could include wearing team colors when they play their rival or rallying around a flag in times of crisis.

To the credit of its creators, *Stranger Things* doesn't deny our duality. It embraces and uses it to play on both our corporeal and existential fears. While the sides of humanity's dual nature aren't seeking to destroy one another, the show does make us somewhat paradoxical with the conflict between our finitude and infinitude, according to Kierkegaard, leading to despair.

## The Left Head—Finitude

*Stranger Things* is full of gross and disgusting reminders that we are mortal and can be killed (and in some cases eaten). As demonstrated in Seasons One and Two, the Demogorgon is one of several dangerous creatures crossing over from the Upside Down that kill humans. We're introduced to this terrible creature at the very beginning of Season One when we see an unnamed Hawkins Lab employee running from and eventually killed by the Demogorgon. The stakes are raised when first Will and then fan favorite Barb Holland are individually attacked and taken to the Upside Down by the Demogorgon. Humans are used to being at the top of the food chain. The realization that there are creatures that are faster, stronger, and possibly more intelligent than we are puts us in a position that we're not accustomed to. We're the prey and not the predator.

We're also treated to glimpses of the Upside Down and are unsettled since it looks like an infected, decayed, and decrepit version of our reality, complete with living black vine tentacles, slime, and particles falling from the sky. This is not a happy place, and even before it happens, we know that things will not end well for Barb. Her death is violent, and disturbing, and we're later grossed out when Joyce and Hopper discover Barb's mutilated and decomposing body covered in a gooey web with a slug-like creature oozing out of her mouth. But we're also disturbed because Barb has become a part of the Upside Down and we fear that Will may soon join her.

The thought of being a host to something, or mutating into something other than *human* makes us more than uncomfortable. The idea of some force infecting our entire world is terrifying. When Joyce and Sheriff Hopper eventually find Will, he is stuck in a disgusting, fleshy organic web with a slimy tentacle down his throat. One month later, back in the "real world," Will is having dinner with his family, but excuses himself to use the restroom, and vomits up a slug-like thing into the sink. This is a harbinger of what's to come in Season Two, in which the Upside Down begins to invade reality, as wherever the Demogorgon goes, the slime spreads. The Upside Down is like an interdimensional disease, spreading from parallel world to parallel world, invading, infecting, and mutating everything, and every*one*, in its path.

## The Right Head—Infinitude

The existence of an alternate dimension challenges our understanding of reality. Structures in Hawkins, such as the Public Library, Castle Byers, and Steve's pool have their "twins" in the Upside Down. There is some kind of a connection linking the *Stranger Things* reality and the Upside Down as actions in the "real world" have an impact on the Upside Down. Joyce hanging Christmas lights in her home enabling communication between her and Will in Season One is a demonstration of this.

Alarmingly, the Upside Down is also home to the Shadow Monster, or Mind Flayer, a creature which demonstrates both its intelligence and malevolence throughout Season Two. An Upside Down populated with demogorgons and demodogs, which seem to be at most semi-intelligent animals, is scary. But an Upside Down that is home to the Shadow Monster, a creature whose power, intellect, and deception is on a par with humans, is terrifying. Humanity's first contact with intelligent life from another world (or dimension) is a classic trope. It shatters the notion that we're unique and special and that scares us because (you guessed it!) we like to believe that we're unique and special. We don't know very much about the Shadow Monster and its beliefs or culture. We do know that it wants to kill us all and is willing to use any tactics at its disposal to achieve its goal. Sound familiar?

At the end of Season Two, we don't yet know whether the Upside Down is a past, future, or an alternate version of Hawkins. What we do know, however, is that the fragile human egos of everyday people couldn't handle the idea of folks being killed by creatures from a parallel "evil" dimension that was discovered through secret government experiments involving children with psionic powers. Could you handle the reality of this kind of knowledge? Or would it seem so fantastic that your armor wouldn't let you accept it? Season Two toys with this notion through a conversation between reporter Murray Bauman, Nancy, and Jonathan. Together they conclude that the reality of what's happened in Hawkins is "too strong" and needs to be "watered down" for it to be accepted by the average person.

## Experiencing Fear from a Vantage Point of Safety

When asked why we love horror fiction, Clive Barker replied that it "shows us that the control we believe we have is purely illusory and that every moment we teeter on chaos and oblivion." Horror fiction allows us to "teeter" on the brink of order and chaos from a vantage point of safety because we know that what is happening on screen isn't real. Horror fiction provides us with a way to safely confront the primal fears that all human beings share from the comfort of our cozy living rooms, couches, and beds. In a way, the screen on our laptop, tablet, phone, or television is both a physical and psychological buffer between the real and mirror fantasy worlds.

Noël Carroll contends that the popularity of horror is "strange" because horror arouses an emotional state that in itself is paradoxical. That is, how can we "enjoy" being in that state of horror when horror appears to be a pretty unpleasant state to be in? Fear is meant to steer us away from terrifying situations—so why do we fire up Netflix and settle in for a long binge of scares? This is certainly a head-scratcher, as according to Carroll, horror arouses two emotions—fear and disgust—that relatively speaking, are pretty unpleasant.

Not only are we afraid of the "monster" (the Demogorgon, the Shadow Monster, Dr. Brenner), but we're also disgusted by it (physical appearance, slime, ooze, the slugs, and the eggs). Yet experiencing fear in a context that is not real and within the safety of our familiar environments can be . . . fun! Furthermore, humans try to avoid disgusting things in real life, but we have no problem viewing them within the context of a horror movie. This could be because there is a fine line between fascination and disgust. Horror addresses our curiosity; it deals with the unthinkable, the unimaginable, the unknown. We get to peek behind the curtain, knowing full well that what we are seeing isn't "real."

Stephen King, the modern-day master of horror, speaks of horror in a similar way. He proposes there are three levels of horror: revulsion, horror, and terror. *Revulsion* is the lowest level in which fear is sparked through disgust that causes viewers to react to what they are seeing physically. There are plenty of instances when *Stranger Things* evokes this level of horror (slime, slugs, and black tentacles).

The second level, *horror*, sparks fear by graphically portraying something that is unbelievable. Viewers react to the abnormality they are seeing. *Stranger Things* is filled with many horrific images: walls stretch, gates open to another dimension, and Eleven confronts the Demogorgon.

King proposes that the highest level is *terror*, which induces fear through imagination. The suggestion of something shocks the viewers into terror. He states, "It is not the physical or mental aberration in itself which horrifies us, but rather the lack of order which these situations seem to imply." This is best exemplified by how the audience can imagine what the Upside Down and the Shadow Monster will do to Hawkins and its residents.

The writers and actors in *Stranger Things* pull us in with interesting and likable characters and take the 1980s nostalgia to an epic level (*Ghostbusters*, Radio Shack, Reagan/Bush yard signs, and The Clash). We are attracted to this world because it's similar enough to the real world, especially for those of us who grew up in the 1980s, for viewers to connect with it. But while we care about Hawkins and the characters who live there, we take comfort in knowing that the bad things that are happening to those characters are not happening to us. After all, unlike the real world, if horror fiction gets to be "too much," we have the power to simply hit the "Back" button and watch something else.

## Making Sense of Real Horror

Fiction has always been a remarkable tool for asking philosophical questions and exploring human life. Fictional characters allow us the luxury of studying various aspects of the human condition without being impeded and overwhelmed by the emotional reality of an actual person. For example, the interaction between the humans and the Shadow Monster could be explored through a lens of interaction and conflict between social or cultural groups. Cultural groups create complex systems involving language, symbols, and norms that extend beyond the self to a social level.

How individuals define, interpret, and react to symbols depends on the cultural significance of those symbols. As such, colors, images, animals, plants, and geographic locations may be significant to different cultures, but for various reasons can result in both real and existential conflict and trauma.

The horrific side of *Stranger Things*, in many ways, serves the same function. It is a venue through which we can explore, unpack, and try to make sense of real horrors without the hang-ups that would come from having to experience them in real life. After all, the likelihood of being kidnapped by monsters, possessed by demons, or mutilated by a Demogorgon is much lower than real-world horrors like childhood leukemia, school shootings, drunk driving accidents, and terrorist attacks.

The closing scene of Season Two, with the Shadow Monster looming threateningly over the Upside Down version of the middle school gym, signals to us that the battle between the real world and the dark forces of the Upside Down are just beginning. Hindsight being 20/20, and since *Stranger Things* takes place in the 1980s, the same thing could be said about the real world horrors that have yet to come. As such, the Shadow Monster becomes symbolic of real-life horrors such as the AIDS epidemic, the Space Shuttle Challenger disaster, the Gulf War, the Opioid Crisis, and 9/11 that have yet to occur and impact the lives of Hawkins's residents.

King believes that the reason horror is so appealing to audiences is due to "the allure of the forbidden." In an interview with Charlie Rose in 1993, King summed this up by saying,

> You are saying to somebody, "Come with me, and I will say things to you that nobody else will say, and I will show you things that nobody dares to show you." . . . Fiction is a lie, but good fiction is the truth inside the lie.

Perhaps the "truth" in the fiction of Stranger Things is that it all seems so familiar to us somehow. Horror allows us to examine issues that we're all aware of but have been forbidden to talk about. *Stranger Things* taps into many things that humans are fearful of—not just the far-reaching philosophical fears covered here of extinction, mutilation, and loss of control—but real fears of losing a child, of being an outcast, and of disappearing and no one caring (Sorry, Barb).

# 6
# The Unique Horror of the Upside Down

WILLIAM C. PAMERLEAU

Barb dangles her feet over the edge of a diving board on a backyard swimming pool, nursing a recent cut which drips blood into the illuminated water below. That blood attracts a monstrous creature, who we briefly see as it lunges at her.

The next time we see Barb, she is waking up, looking disheveled and spitting out brown mucus, at the bottom of the same pool. Except it's not the same pool. There's no water. Instead its surfaces are covered with thick, vine-like tendrils. It's lit with a bluish light, neither day nor night—an unnatural twilight, sprinkled with white spores that float about. The eerie scene takes on a different quality as she notices the monster lurking in the corner, which, now that Barb is up, decides it's had enough waiting around and is ready to eat. Barb runs for the pool ladder, and almost makes it out before being pulled back to her evident demise in a shot very reminiscent of a desperate swimmer being pulled beneath the surface in the movie *Jaws*.

This is one of our first views of the Upside Down, the parallel dimension that is the source of the horror threatening the town of Hawkins in *Stranger Things*. It's a frightening scene for two very different reasons. First, the surroundings Barb finds herself in when she awakens have an uncanny feel. In one way she's right where she was before the creature attacked. She's in the very same pool, but it's transformed in a sinister way. And she seems to be the only person in this place, as her friend Nancy does not respond to her calls for help. Though, of course she's not entirely alone; there is the monster, which is the second reason the scene is so frightening. There's something out to get her, and we watch with a good deal of suspense, wondering if she can get away.

These two elements—the eerie, haunting environment of the Upside Down and the vicious creatures that inhabit it—are intertwined in the narrative but offer very different sorts of horror experience. While the monsters deliver the most urgent threat and the most intensive scares, the Upside Down itself adds a quality that is far more unique. It's obviously unsettling, but in a subtle way that is difficult to put your finger on. With the aid of some existentialist philosophy, however, I think I can reveal why the Upside Down has the effect it does. And if you haven't yet been sufficiently creeped out by the Upside Down, this discussion will make sure that you are.

## What Is the Upside Down?

The quick answer: an alternate but parallel dimension. Will disappears to someplace, and Eleven explains to Will's friends where he is by flipping over a game board and pointing to the underside. Like the Demogorgon and the Mind Flayer, the boys use their Dungeons & Dragons lore to make sense of what Eleven is suggesting. I find this a clever strategy: since being young and spending so much time in fantasy worlds, the boys are far more willing to consider alternative dimensions as plausible explanation than the adults (who will require far more tangible evidence).

Editing techniques encourage us to buy the D&D explanation. Dustin reads the following description of an alternate dimension from the game's lore:

> The Veil of Shadows is a dimension that is a dark reflection or echo of our world. It is a place of decay and death. A plane out of phase, a place of monsters. It is right next to you and you don't even see it.

As he reads, the scene intermittently cuts to Chief Hopper who is exploring the lab, where the gate to the Upside Down has been opened. This clearly implies that Dustin is describing the very place that Hopper is approaching.

So the Upside Down is an alternate dimension, described as sickly—a place of death. At the same time, it is an image of our world. As we get glimpses of what it's like (as in the scene with Barb described above), we find that the places and structures are largely the same as in the real world. As Hopper and Joyce track the Demogorgon to its lair in the Upside Down (the public library), they pass through a downtown area that has parked cars, business signs, and the rest.

But of course it's not exactly a replica, as the Upside Down has no people or any sort of living thing that we would expect in the real world. It does nonetheless have its own biology: the living tendrils that cover the surfaces, the floating, ash-like spores, and of course the monsters. The Upside Down, then, is dead with respect to familiar, earthly life, but quite alive with respect to its own other worldly biota.

It's also mysterious, and sometimes downright puzzling. For one thing, images of the Upside-Down contain curious details that you might not notice in a first viewing but, thinking back on them, raise questions. For instance, in the Upside-Down version of Will's fort there is a hand-drawn picture on the wall, and in the Upside Down middle school there are flyers on the wall. But there are no people walking around drawing pictures or pinning fliers. How did they get there? How do any of these sorts of details come about?

In the final scene of Season Two, the camera rotates so as to seemingly break the ground surface and re-emerge in the Upside Down. We begin the scene viewing the outside of the real-world middle school and end with the same vantage point on the Upside Down middle school, and with much of the same details including cars parked out front and the decorative lighting strung for the dance going on inside. (Apparently there is electricity in the Upside Down.) If it's a reflection of the real world at that level of detail, why don't we see changes occurring: lights stringing themselves or cars driving themselves? Similarly, the trees seem dead, so how did they get to the size they are now?

If you pay attention to these details, you'll find several other seeming inconsistencies. And at one level, that's just what they seem to be. The series creators, Matt and Ross Duffer, more or less admit this. Ross explains in their 2017 interview with Vulture "We're believers that you can get so caught up on the logic of all this stuff that you end up going nowhere. Sometimes it's as simple as, 'Well, that's cool,' and you just keep pushing forward." But wait, it *is* another dimension, after all, and one we do not know much about. Its very mysteriousness allows us to suspend suspicions of what seem like narrative flaws by acknowledging that this place might operate according to quite different physical laws than our own.

In the same interview, Matt explains, "in terms of horror, it's scarier when you don't fully understand what's happening. If you were to encounter something from another world or dimension, it would be beyond comprehension . . . the weirder it is, the more inexplicable it is, the scarier it is." Personally, I'm good with that. I'm willing to shrug my shoulders and take the fact that the other dimension is unexplainable as the reason why I can't explain it. And as we'll see, that very mysteriousness, as Matt suggests, helps explain the horror.

## Monsters

Why is the Upside Down scary? The obvious reason is that it has monsters. In Season One we have the Demogorgon, who abducts people and takes them to the Upside Down public library where, apparently, they are eventually eaten. The Demogorgon's cousins in Season Two, however, are apt to just eat people where they find them. (Recall the fate of Bob Newby as he tries to escape the lab.) These creatures provide the most immediate physical threat throughout both seasons. But there are also tendrils that entwine the unwary, as they do to Hopper as he explores the tunnels beneath Hawkins, and spores that can sicken people or leave them unconscious (which also happens to the ever-suffering Hopper).

Philosopher Noël Carroll has suggested in *The Philosophy of Horror* that our fascination with monsters is in part because they violate standing categories: "They are disturbing and disgusting, but, at the same time, they are also objects of fascination—again, just because they transgress standing categories of thought." This is in part applicable to the monsters of the Upside Down. As mysterious entities from another dimension, they absolutely transgress standing categories, creating a *what-the-hell-is-that?* reaction in the viewer.

But let's face it, these monsters drive the horror element by providing suspense and jump scares. Movies like *Jaws* and *Alien* seem to be the show's spiritual precursors, and it's easy to read the imagery as an homage to this sort of horror. The jump scare is a tried-and-true tactic, but for that reason it's also not terribly original. I do not mean this as a criticism, however . . . the suspense and thrills are done well and are a significant part of the enjoyment of the series. I would not argue with someone who claims that this is, in fact, the show's most horrifying aspect.

The Mind Flayer is a different sort of monster entirely, and the sort of threat it poses in Season Two is correspondingly different. Despite its awesome and menacing appearance, it doesn't seem to pose a direct physical threat, but it is rather a sinister intelligence, apparently with plans for Will, Hawkins, and maybe the whole world. It possesses Will, and through him is able to understand and manipulate the actions of the human beings out to stop it. Unlike the animal-like "demodogs" (as Dustin dubs them), we wonder about the Mind Flayer's goals and strategies. The effect on the viewer is to produce worry as much as suspense, amplified by that mysteriousness which pervades the Upside Down.

Here again, however, we have a rather familiar horror narrative: the sinister mastermind with malevolent intentions towards the protagonists, whose plans are shrouded in mystery until they are unveiled in the course of the story. The villains that propel the stories in superhero and James Bond movies, for example, provide similar threats (although the Upside Down is so steeped in mystery that we may never discover the full intentions of its intelligent denizens). Again, though, the claim that this type of narrative is unoriginal is not intended as a criticism of *Stranger Things*, and in fact genre conventions can be of great use in the hands of talented artists who can manipulate expectations of how the genre is supposed to work in order to achieve the desired effect in the viewers.

My point here is that as successful as the monsters are in the *Stranger Things* narrative, they are not what gives the series its unique quality as horror cinema. It is, rather, the very nature of the Upside Down itself.

# Being Human

The Upside Down is unnerving because it appeals to a fundamental aspect of human experience: the fact that our sense of self is determined by the world that shapes our identity. Confronted with what appears to be our world, but isn't, the Upside Down evokes a tension between the familiar and alien—a sensation that strikes to the very heart of human experience.

To appreciate my point, we need to lay out some philosophy: specifically, the views of the twentieth-century German philosopher Martin Heidegger as put forth in his *Being and Time*. Heidegger pointed out that our type of being—human being—is fundamentally different than the existence of the objects we deal with in the world. At one level, this is quite obvious, but Heidegger points out aspects of our experience that we are not immediately aware of but have profound implications.

To begin with, the nature of our experience is to exist *in relation to* the world. Heidegger refers to human existence as *Dasein*, which is translated literally as "being there." We always find ourselves in a certain place and time, a certain point of history, involved in some specific set of practices and norms. The particular way in which we are situated makes us who we are. We don't just exist as some independent, self-contained thing; we are always being *there*.

Heidegger refers to this aspect of us as "being-in-the-world." He doesn't just mean that we find ourselves part of a culture or country. That's obviously true, but his point is that our very sense of self comes from our relation to the world. Think about your everyday experience of things. When we encounter objects, we do not think of them in some objective, detached way; we experience them in terms of their functions, purposes, and significance for our plans. When you see a hammer, for example, you don't think "There's a piece of metal, rounded at one end and forked on the other, with a piece of wood sticking out of the middle of it." You see a hammer, a tool, a thing that's used to pound nails. You may not consciously think "nail pounder" to yourself, but you are immediately aware of the way it serves that and other purposes. Your familiarity with carpentry lurks in the background, making the metal and wood thing stand out *as* a hammer, and not just a metal-and-wood thing. On the other hand, if you had no knowledge of carpentry or this type of tool, you would experience the thing differently. You wouldn't see it as a thing to pound nails with, and maybe all you would think is "There's a piece of metal, rounded at one end and forked on the other, with a piece of wood sticking out of the middle of it."

So when we become aware of things in the world, we see them as serving this purpose or that, and there's a whole web of interrelated functions and expectations that make us aware of everything in context. What's more, our identity, our sense of self, is just the collection of all these ways of relating to and interpreting the world around us. So on the one hand, I reveal the various things in the world as having the meaning they do because I understand their social context and history; and on the other hand I think of *myself* in terms of how I relate to all these functions and purposes. If, like Chief Hopper, I am a sheriff in a small town, then I perceive and interpret the world according to my functions as a protector of citizens, investigator of crimes, and so forth. While others might not even notice the furtive behavior of the guy in the alley, I would immediately see him as a potential perpetrator and myself as a potential source of intervention in a crime.

We interpret the world this way largely because we're socialized into it—we inherit the meanings of things from others. But we don't think in terms of specific others, but in a collective, vague sense which Heidegger refers to as the *they*. It's similar to what is meant when someone remarks, "You know what they say." In general, we act as *they* expect us to act, and determine the meaning and use of things as *they* have already determined them. We may not be immediately aware of how the *they* shape our experience of the world, but the attitude of the *they* informs most of our perceptions of what things in the world are, what social roles are, and what we are as part of this larger, interconnected whole. Being-in-the-world, then, means we have internalized the meanings and expectations of the *they*.

Let's consider what Will's normal, everyday experience is like. He's a middle-school student in a small rural town in the Midwest. He lives in a house with his mother and brother, and plays with his friends in the neighborhood and woods near his home. All of these locations are filled with things whose purpose is immediately obvious and familiar: forts, bicycles, school back packs, and bedroom furniture. His home is perhaps the central location, as it is for all of us: a place where everything is very familiar and central to his day-to-day functions. He is himself at home, where he relates to everything immediately and effortlessly. And his involvement with all these things, places, and activities makes him who he is. Finally, particularly because he is young, Will takes all of this for granted as the world provided by the undifferentiated attitude of the *they*. Things are as *they* have determined them to be.

## Lost in the Upside Down

Consider now what it would be like for Will to find himself in a place that in one sense is the place he has grown up in, but in another sense isn't even close. How disconcerting must that be, given that Will's sense of self is directly connected to that world?

We don't get to see Will's adventures in the Upside Down directly until just before the Demogorgon finds him hiding in his (parallel dimension) fort in the woods. But he makes contact with his mother by interacting with the lights in the real-world house somehow (another mysterious aspect of the Upside Down). We also know from various other scenes, most occurring later in the series, what the Upside Down is like. So let's now reconstruct what Will must have experienced upon finding himself transported to this other dimension.

His first impression must be that he's still in the world. Why wouldn't he be? Everything looks the same in terms of where things are: the same houses, streets, trees, and etc. He is likely to react by asking "What has happened to the world?" as opposed to concluding that he is in some other dimension. But he quickly finds that the world doesn't function like it should, and that is largely because there is no one else there, at least no other human beings. No one answers his calls. If the phone works, there is no one to pick up on the other end, but it's likely that much of the equipment he encounters won't work at all if it's a replica and not the real thing. No trusted authority figure is there to help. The taken-for-granted world that he comfortably trusted in the hands of the *they* is suddenly meaningless when *they* are not there.

Where does Will go in this perverted world? Home, of course. On one level, that seems a futile gesture, since his mother and brother are not there to help, and nothing probably functions as it should. But Will, since he is *Dasein* (being-in-the-world) is so constituted by that orientation that he would be unable to envision any other obvious option (which is how most anyone would react in his position). The fact that the Upside Down is a replica of his own world immediately triggers his engrained expectations of what those things mean. He cannot help but experience the familiar places differently than what a lifetime of experience has accustomed him to, even if at the same time it's all terribly wrong. When Will's mother Joyce makes contact via the household electronics, it's in Will's room, where he goes because his experience of place suggests to him that this is the place he should go.

Imagine being in the place that *feels* in every fiber of your being like the center of your universe and have it be so utterly alien at the same time. Will is in one sense at home, but in another he is far away. The irony of this experience of place reaches its crescendo when Joyce pleads with Will to tell him where he is, and Will, communicating with lights aligned with the letters of the alphabet, spells out "R-I-G-H-T H-E-R-E"!

## The Unique Creepy of the Upside Down

Let's apply Heidegger's concepts directly to this situation by comparing waking up in our own world and waking up in the Upside Down in terms of being-on-the-world. You get up in the morning with a sense of what your obligations are for the day: getting to work, attending school, visiting your sick grandmother, and so forth. And those activities are understood in terms of larger contexts like earning a promotion, getting a degree, or satisfying the demands of your family. You must first navigate a world of objects like coffee pots, toasters, and toothbrushes, and later a car, bus, or metro, and so on throughout the day. These interactions are a part of you, and in that sense you yourself extend out into the world, both in terms of space and time. You leave home already anticipating the drive into town *where* you work, and you feverishly work today to finish tasks required for the conference next week, your immediate *future*.

Now imagine you wake up in a world like the Upside Down. The things you interact with are still there, and your immediate response is to expect all of the same sort of interactions that you're accustomed to. It is the fact that these things are the instruments by which you pursue your meaningful goals and purposes which makes them significant in the first place. But those connections are broken because the world is essentially dead. So here are all these places and things which immediately call forth in us a way of interacting, but we cannot interact with them. That juxtaposition between the familiar yet estranged creates a dissonance that would be, if you were there, extremely unsettling. And as we experience this vicariously through the characters of *Stranger Things,* we experience something similar, which is precisely the series' unique horror element.

Confronting the bodily remains of someone close to us may be analogous to the experience I'm trying to describe. If you've ever been to an open-casket funeral of someone you've known well, you might have had the unsettling experience of seeing the person you spent so much time with and always expected certain reactions from, and now being unable to interact with them at all. Hearing of the person's death is one thing, and you may completely accept that she or he has passed on and is no longer with us. But seeing the body is something else, because that familiar face so readily brings to mind all the ways in which you have interacted with that person in the past. It seems like the person should sit up and begin talking, as has always happened before; and your knowledge that that won't happen amplifies the loss.

Similarly, if we return to a place where we had once spent a lot of time, we get an odd sensation that is a juxtaposition of old familiar feelings and memories with all the changes that have occurred since. This might happen if you return to a childhood home after years of absence: part of you expects to see your childhood friends round the corner from the house you grew up in, while another part of you is conscious that the new owners have added an addition to the place and painted it a different color. And this is very different from just remembering your childhood home while you're still miles away or reminiscing with your family. Being with those things in that place brings forth the reactions that are still a part of you, even though you know that you are shut off from those past connections. In the presence of deceased friends or places from our distant past, the sense of loss is heightened by the fact that these things evoke an expectation of interaction that we know must go unanswered.

The Upside Down evokes a heightened sense of this experience. Imagining a place that is like the place we are in right now, right here, but severed from meaningful interactions, creates a heightened sense of loss of the world and a perversion of our own way of existing.

Consider how different *Stranger Things* would be if the other dimension were fundamentally unlike our own. Imagine it to be like the surface of an alien planet. Maybe it has some odd geological features and its own flora and fauna. Will is lost in this dimension, let's say, and instead of returning "home," he has to find some cubbyhole to hide from the monsters that lurk there, or fashion weapons out of the resources he finds. This might be an interesting and terrifying narrative device, but it would be a rather familiar narrative, and it would be completely different than the experience of the Upside Down.

Compare two scenes: Joyce and Hopper looking for Will in the final episode of Season One of *Stranger Things*, and the scene at the beginning of *Alien* where the crew is exploring an alien ship. I do not know if this was the intent, but the former scene definitely evoked the latter to me. Joyce and Hopper are in hazmat suits with illuminated helmets that look similar to the space suits of the crew from *Alien*. When Joyce and Hopper find Will, they pull out some long worm-like thing from his esophagus, reminiscent of the face-grabber that attaches itself to a member of the crew in *Alien*. And the dark, silent atmosphere is certainly similar in both scenes, as is the overall mood of exploration and suspense about what might be found.

The big difference is the environment: the scene in *Alien* takes place against the backdrop of a large, wholly unfamiliar alien ship; the scene in *Stranger Things* takes place inside the town library, which we know from previous episodes. An alien world provides a certain mystery and horror based on the fact that it's totally unknown. But imposing the alien on our own world provides a juxtaposition between the familiar and its perversion that creates an uncanny experience. You may or may not find the latter experience more frightening than the former, but the Upside Down's ability to draw on the very nature of our human experience provides an unsettling sensation that should be savored by fans of the genre.

# III

## Nothing Is Stranger than Reality

# 7
# The Mind Flayer through a Gnostic Lens

JEFFREY A. EWING

In Season Two, the gang find themselves encountering an entity—dubbed the Mind Flayer—that operates unlike any living entity the world has ever seen. In the heart of the Upside Down it sits, an otherworldly tendriled shadow controlling and manipulating anything that lives there, its reach extending even into our own dimension. We don't *really* know its nature, but what we do know is shocking—how can we understand its power, its intelligence, or its relation to the Upside Down, a dark copy of our own world? One philosophical legacy in particular may give insight into our understanding of both a created, derivative world and an entity at its center that has a godlike role at its center—the *Demiurge*, a concept that influenced the thinking of both Plato, the Neoplatonists, and the Gnostics who sought to make sense of our world.

## How Many Minds Could a Mind Flayer Flay If a Mind Flayer Could Flay Minds?

In *Stranger Things*, the citizens of Hawkins, Indiana, find themselves threatened by the Upside Down, a dimension that's a dark reflection of our own world down to its physical constructed objects—schools, tree houses, pools, you name it. We don't know exactly how the Upside Down works—its origin, the extent of what lives there, or why it has copies of human-made buildings, for example. Yet, Season Two adds a very significant detail that helps our understanding of this creepy mirror world: we now know the shadowy Mind Flayer has, as far as we can tell, telepathically infected and controlled the creatures of the Upside Down and can infect and manipulate entities in other dimensions (like Will). Will discusses the Shadow Monster's influence in his own body:

> It's like I feel what the shadow monster's feeling. See what he's seeing. Like in the Upside Down? Some of him is there. But some of him is here, too. —Here, like, in this house?—In this house and in me. It's like It's like he's reaching into Hawkins more and more. And the more he spreads, the more connected to him I feel. ("Dig Dug")

As the gang discuss ("The Mind Flayer"):

> **MIKE:** Okay, so, the shadow monster's inside everything. And if the vines feel something like pain, then so does Will.
>
> **LUCAS:** And so does Dart.
>
> **MIKE:** Yeah. Like what Mr. Clarke taught us. The hive mind.
>
> **STEVE:** Hive mind?
>
> **DUSTIN:** A collective consciousness. It's a super-organism.
>
> **MIKE:** And this is the thing that controls everything. It's the brain.
>
> **DUSTIN:** Like the Mind Flayer.

The Mind Flayer, also known as the Shadow Monster, has the ability to infect and control everything in the Upside Down. Its control even extends into our world, controlling across dimensions. In short, it is intelligent, incorporeal, and a grave threat to the autonomy of all life it comes in contact with.

The Mind Flayer, its features looking more like smoke with sentience and shape than like anything on our world, lives (if you can call it that) in the Upside Down, a topsy-turvy shadow world that echoes our own. We don't know its exact relationship to the Upside Down. As far as we know it has enveloped life there, but we don't know the extent of its control there (or even the extent of the Upside Down itself), the origin of the Upside Down, or whether the Mind Flayer had anything to do with its generation. We also don't know how it originated, if it's the only one of its kind, or how it sustains itself. We do, however, know that it has a strong desire to expand and control all life it comes in contact with.

As explained further by Dustin in "The Mind Flayer":

NANCY: Okay, this Mind Flamer . . .

DUSTIN: Flayer, Mind Flayer.

NANCY: . . . What does it want?

DUSTIN: To conquer us, basically. It believes it's the master race.

STEVE: Like the Germans.

DUSTIN: The Nazis?

STEVE: Yeah, yeah the Nazis.

DUSTIN: If the Nazis were from another dimension . . . it views other races, like us, as inferior to itself.

MIKE: It wants to spread, take over other dimensions.

Whatever the origins of the Upside Down (and the Mind Flayer's connection to it), it either has already spread to other dimensions or, upon discovering our world, plans to take over and is capable of such expansion. Once in a dimension it can control all the entities it encounters within it in a sort of hive mind, giving them co-ordinated commands and the ability to share, to a certain extent, thoughts, feelings, and the like. In the Upside Down, the strange duplicate world that is modeled after our own, this makes the Mind Flayer the master of that realm, potentially its origin and at least its controller.

What makes this so interesting is that the Upside Down is a crude, dark, but still somewhat detailed version of our own world. We never see how buildings like Castle Byers or the school become copied—are they mysteriously built by invisible hands as their Earthly counterparts are? Do they periodically manifest? We have no idea. They are detailed, slimy, dark variants of their counterpart architecture in our world, and it is possible to connect to our dimension from there. Moreover, they are devoid of humans (excepting when we break the barrier and enter there)—but not their own domestic, dangerous life. And at the center, pulling the strings—the Mind Flayer, an incorporeal psionic entity, the nigh-all-powerful ruler of a derivative reality that's a mere reflection of our own. Philosophically, if that sounds familiar it's because it is . . .

## Thus Spake the Demiurge

Philosophically, the concept of the Demiurge began as mentioned in the works of Plato before filtering into Neoplatonist and Gnostic thought over time (with wildly divergent interpretations at parts). The term 'demiurge' (*dêmiourgos,* means 'artisan' or 'craftsman'), signifying a creator entity responsible for the creation of the physical world as we know it. The concept emerged first in Plato's dialogue *Timaeus* (around 360 B.C.E.); the Demiurge is portrayed as a benevolent being who "fashioned and shaped" the material world. For Plato, the world exhibits a beautiful order that signals the work of a divine Craftsman, and it is this Craftsman who took disordered matter in its state of primordial chaos and imposed order on it, creating the beautiful, calculable universe we experience.

In creating the physical, observable material universe, the Demiurge used the model of the eternal, perfect and intangible world beyond the physical—that is, the Forms, the perfect and unchanging ideas or categories that all existing things approximate. For Plato, there existed a layer of existence beyond and behind reality, unchanging and perfect, composed of ideal variants of the objects and ideas we know. These Forms, being perfect, are never present in the material world, but rather the material world reflects and is an imperfect approximation of the Forms. Here lies the handiwork of Plato's Demiurge, then, the creative power behind our imperfect material world, itself reflecting the realm of the Forms as a derivative and imperfect version, an echo.

## Neoplatonism

Following the works and developing the philosophies of Plato, Neoplatonism, founded by Plotinus (204–270 C.E.), carried over a number of concepts from the Platonic corpus. Notably, this includes a variation on Plato's dialogue around the Demiurge and its role in the creation of the material world. For Plotinus, the ultimate intelligence behind existence (both physical and beyond) is the One, the central intelligent source behind all things. The Demiurge served as a secondary creator deity, if you will, in effect emulating the One through its role in shaping the material world. Like Plato, Plotinus held that material reality was indeed generated by the Demiurge, but Plotinus specified the nature of that creation. In his account, the Demiurge did not actually create the material world, but rather imposed a sensible form on passive, inert matter. The Demiurge, itself a reflection or emulation, thus shaped this inert matter based on an emulation of the One and its role in the creation of the Forms.

As in Plato, we arrive at an imperfect realm that reflects ultimate reality. The Demiurge itself is good, and any imperfections in the material world result from its inevitably imperfect material components. Plotinus's work, following Plato, was composed in part to specifically repudiate more negative views of the Demiurge. According to Plotinus, the Demiurge, despite its inadequacies or the inadequacies of its source material, really tries to serve the true God and to create a beautiful and well-ordered material world, and truly has respect for the perfect spiritual realm.

## Gnosticism

Whereas the account of the Demiurge from Plato through the Neoplatonists held to an overall positive view of the Demiurge, attributing beneficence to it while blaming imperfections in the world on necessary flaws in matter itself, early *Gnostic* thinkers took a much harsher view in their own conceptualizations of the Demiurge. Gnostics had various forms, with no single tradition or teaching, but there is an overall pattern to their way of thinking. Broadly speaking, Gnostics believed that a highest, unknowable supreme being was behind all reality—a perfect, all-good entity governing a perfect spiritual order. By contrast, the material world is created and governed by a Demiurge who is at best incompetent and at worst evil.

Beyond these similarities, the historical variations between diverging Gnostic sects created a web of divergent interpretations of the nature of the material world and, correspondingly, different understandings of the Demiurge. All forms of Gnosticism held the Demiurge to be inferior to God. According to the Gnostic Valentinus, for example, the Demiurge (identified with the god worshipped in Israel) created the material world from primordial chaos. In this account, the Demiurge was broadly considered extremely just but imperfect. For example, the Valentinian *Tripartite Tractate* describes the Demiurge, as a purposeful creation of the true God that seeks to fulfill its duties:

> He is the lord of all of them, that is, the countenance which the logos (Sophia) brought forth in his thought as a representation of the Father of the Totalities. Therefore, he is adorned with every name which is a representation of him, since he is characterized by every property and glorious quality. For he too is called 'father' and 'god' and 'demiurge' and 'king' and 'judge' and 'place' and 'dwelling' and 'law'. (*Tripartite Tractate* 100:21–30)

By contrast, another major tradition in Gnosticism, known as the Sethian Gnostics, held a much darker view of the Demiurge and its role in the universe.

Emerging in the second century C.E. as a fusion of distinct Hellenistic Judaic philosophies, Sethians held that an Unknown God created a succession of male and female *aeons* that together compose the *Pleroma*, the totality of the physical universe. Some versions have the Aeon Sophia create a being known as the *Yaldabaoth*, a serpent with a lion's head, that is the artisan, the Platonic Demiurge, that steals divine power and created the material world in imitation of the Pleroma. This Demiurge falsely claimed himself to be the only God, the creator identified in *Genesis*, and creates the first humans (Adam and Eve) from remaining divine power.

In this account, the Demiurge, *Yaldabaoth*, is a false god presenting itself as the true God, and is the source of deception and evil. Consequently, all his creation—the entire material world—is evil. Moreover, the laws it passed down, the laws codified in the Ten Commandments and elsewhere, are then held to be evil . . . and for some Gnostics in this tradition, their moral duty became to oppose these precepts and wage war on the Creator.

This variant of Gnosticism, then, portrayed the Demiurge as power-hungry, blasphemous, and antagonistic to the true God, to spiritual order, and to the best interests of humankind. The Demiurge wants nothing less than to have ultimate control. With all these variations of the Demiurge account before us, which is the most insightful for the Upside Down's own potential Demiurge, the Mind Flayer?

## More Like the Shadow *Mobster*, Amirite?

In Platonic and Gnostic traditions, the Demiurge created reality as a mere reflection of ultimate reality. By contrast, we don't know what caused or created the Upside Down or its ability to duplicate the real world—it could be the creation of the Mind Flayer, the product of the experiments at the Hawkins National Laboratory, or a realm that has no relation to either of those potential explanations.

Without knowing its origins, we obviously can't really know how the Mind Flayer relates to them or, specifically, whether it had a role in the creation of the Upside Down . . . so a key element of our puzzle is missing. Simultaneously, the question is currently open . . . we don't know that the Mind Flayer didn't have a role in its creation or continued maintenance so the question definitely isn't precluded. So we can discuss what it would mean for that to be true—that is, to discuss the meaning of a relationship between the Mind Flayer and the Upside Down.

And that relationship *is* plausible from what we do know. The Upside Down mysteriously mimics our own, and not even merely with regard to our world's physical features. Rather, we know that it contains replicas of manmade objects—Castle Byers, pools, the school, and so on. We know these features stay relatively up to date, although we haven't seen them changing in response to our own construction and changes. The Upside Down is a detailed reflection of our own built world, much in the way that all accounts of the Demiurge posit that it created the material world as an imperfect reflection of the actual world, the spiritual world beyond that contains the only *true* essence. And the world *is* imperfect—it is cold where our world is warm and perpetually dusk or night (with falling spores) where our world is sunny and diverse. Where our world has people and adorable animals of every stripe, we've seen the Upside Down beset with dangerous beasts (no humans to be seen) and the only adorable animals we've seen are but early stages of these dangerous beasts. As far as worlds go, what we can see is an Upside Down that is dangerous, ugly, derivative, and (perhaps worse) close enough to our own to be truly disturbing. An imperfect reflection indeed.

At the same time we've seen evidence that the Mind Flayer has expanded to control all life in the Upside Down. It can possess entities of very diverse makeups, and with that possession connect to and control them (from demodogs to humans). This is a godlike ability to control, as it can control many creatures simultaneously with no visible effort, and its level of connection is so deep that pain in the body of its puppets hurts it. Moreover, it is incorporeal yet takes form at will, appearing as a non-physical smoke monster that can appear out of nowhere, take a form, and turn back into a sentient fog just as fast. It is truly unlike anything on our version of Earth. From the party's conversations we can infer that it wants to spread into and control other worlds than its own, which may mean it moves from reality to reality in a gambit for total control and the Upside Down is where we first encountered it, or it may mean that it started in the Upside Down and desires to destroy and subjugate humanity and conquer our realm now that it has discovered it. Either way, it is vastly powerful, unlike anything we've experienced, and seeks to conquer our world—the *real* reality—and upend its dominant species, us.

Here's one clue to help us answer not only *whether* it's like the Demiurge but rather *which* version of the Demiurge it may be most like. We're looking at, essentially, three different versions of the Demiurge. First, the Demiurge of Plato and the Neoplatonists is an ultimately good, if flawed, servant of the true God or operating principles of the universe. Think of it as the loyal younger brother mimicking its older, better, more talented brother: it isn't good at *anything* the older brother does but that's not from malice, opposition, or bad intent. On the other hand, of the spectrum of Gnostic interpretations we have some that align moderately well with the Platonic interpretation: the Demiurge is a good but imperfect servant of the ultimate God, sometimes less competently portrayed than the Platonic interpretation but a servant of the ultimate God and a respectful mimic of true reality. Finally, the Sethian Gnostic tradition held the Demiurge to be some degree of evil, a pretender to the godly throne who created a material world as a replica of the real reality yet with desires for absolute control and in opposition to the real world (and the true God that governs it).

With this contrast before us, the Mind Flayer comes clearer into view as to the Demiurge variant it is more likely to be. Its relationship to *real* reality isn't one of respect or deference, but rather opposition—the Mind Flayer wants absolute control over our world, and it *hates* any threats to its dominance that stem from the real world. It appears to hate or resent Eleven, the arty, or anyone responsible for its expulsion from our realm. Rather than respect this world and its power, the Mind Flayer cannot accept a world that isn't within its orbit. And with all the entities under its control, they're used to destroying life in the 'real world' rather than serving or protecting it. The Mind Flayer isn't stupid or incompetent . . . it's antagonistic to our species and all life on this planet. Sethian 'evil' Demiurge it is.

## The Dark Demiurge

We can't say for certain that the Mind Flayer *is* the Demiurge . . . we have no idea what the Upside Down exactly is, how it mirrors our world, or how it came into being. We don't know where the Mind Flayer comes from, whether it created the Upside Down or the creatures in it, or whether it's creating the structures in a conscious reflection of the real world (or whether they change on their own, or something else changes them . . .). The best we can do is speculate based on available evidence, and we certainly don't know the Mind Flayer didn't create the Upside Down, so the exploration is worth our time.

Just as, for all accounts of the Demiurge, it is the ruler of a world that's a flawed reflection of our own, the Mind Flayer rules a world that reflects our own but a world with entirely different species, and a darker, more dangerous, less complete world at that. While we don't know whether it created the Upside Down or the species in it, we do know its rule is far more complete than that of the Demiurge . . . the latter may desire dominance, but it does not control everything in its purview. And we know it does have the same absolute desire for control that characterizes the Demiurge in its darkest interpretation: the Sethian Demiurge wants to be the true God and control all, including ultimate reality, same as the Mind Flayer. On this front, it bears a number of similarities.

So we have a realm, the Upside Down, that is a dark and imperfect reflection of the real world. Similarly, from Plato to Plotinus to the Gnostics, the material world is but a reflection of the real ultimate reality, ranging from an imperfect mirror to an evil duplicate. And they are both ruled by a powerful entity that desires to rule and control all life, and simultaneously has contempt for the real reality alongside living beings that populate it (and any challenges to their own power). We may not know whether or not the Mind Flayer did create the Upside Down, but we know it functions the same within it. The Mind Flayer *is* (likely) the Demiurge, and the Upside Down Reality is its false, mirror realm.

*Our* realm, rather than being the false-material-world of Platonic and Gnostic theorizing, is the *real* world then, the ultimate reality. Technically the real world could be a mirror itself, sure, but it remains more real than the derivative Upside Down. What would that make the residents of Hawkins? Gods? Angels? We really have no way of knowing.

But we know that the Mind Flayer may well be the long fabled Demiurge, and the story confirms the most evil interpretation of the Demiurge: an evil being playing at being God.

# 8
# In Eggos We Trust

CHRIS WIGLEY

Cast your mind back to the end of Season One and all the heartache and feels that came with it. Remember the streaming tears and how you wiped your nose on your sleeve between long, snotty sobs. We lost El . . . in an act of true heroism, she sacrificed herself to save her friends. El wasn't just the hero Hawkins needed, she was the hero Hawkins deserved.

Before you fly the Team Eleven flag once more, consider this: you got it wrong. El isn't the real hero of *Stranger Things*. Sure, she's a psionic beacon of badassery, but there are greater powers stirring quietly in the background, powers that transcend even dimensions hitherto unimagined by the characters of *Stranger Things*. These powers aren't hidden, they've been there all along and you just haven't noticed. Hawkins's salvation won't be found in the hands of a super-powered tween, but in a golden beacon of hope and friendship. *Eggos* will save Hawkins.

## There's Nothing Simple about It

*Stranger Things* offers us a skewed take on a familiar world. It's a vision of 1980s America smeared with nostalgic tropes, and occasional continuity errors (that Demogorgon miniature wasn't released until the middle of 1984). The small town of Hawkins is a cosy recreation of the America many remember, even those of us who weren't there. Before all hell breaks loose and people whose names begin with "B" start getting killed, our ramshackle party of nerds, namely Mike, Lucas, Dustin, and Will, spend their days playing Dungeons & Dragons, riding bikes, and fumbling through the early stages of adolescence.

We've all been there. The zits and body hair, the anxiety and heartache, all those painful things that go hand-in-hand with puberty. It's a time of transition between the simplicity of childhood and the complexities of the adult world. Those vanilla facts you learned from Mom and Dad are obliterated by sex ed class and the death of your first pet. All of a sudden nothing makes sense. There are no happy endings. Dad can't love Mom if he's sleeping with the cleaner. Jesus lost to science. Everything you held as real falls apart at the seams. Your parents lied. The world isn't how they told you it is.

## You Shouldn't Like Things because People Tell You You're Supposed To

Teen angst and mood swings aside, the idea of false realities isn't as strange as it might first seem. In the early 1980s the French philosopher Jean Baudrillard pondered this. He theorized that we experience the world through a type of mutual mass hallucination. Rather than running with the cosmic acid orgy connotations, he suggested that booms in consumer culture, capitalism, and technology have reshaped us, masking whatever *was* real behind symbols and representations. Baudrillard called this *hyperreality*, the "generation by models of a real without origin or reality." Put more simply, it's *an inability to distinguish reality from fiction.*

Differentiating reality from fiction doesn't mean hyperreality is a form of medical psychosis. In this sense, the idea of the real is the essence of a thing *prior* to any instances that alter its intention or meaning; the zit before the makeup (or before the airbrush). Baudrillard described this in terms of models—essentially copies or generations of what came before. To understand the idea of a generation of models, we'll turn to the ever-debated fan favorite, Barb.

One day a photo is taken of Barb at school. There is nothing unusual about this picture. It captures the visual Barbness of Barb. To a stranger it communicates, among other things, but most generally, teenager, high school, glasses, red head, and dork. When Barb disappears and the citizens of Hawkins make missing persons posters, they use the same picture. All of a sudden, the grainy Xeroxed face of Barb now means something else. It's no longer the essence of a teenager in school, but a visual identifier showing the face of a missing person. The fact Barb is in high school and is a dork is less relevant than the fact she is a teenager, has glasses, and red hair. These are the features we must identify. Her status in school is irrelevant.

Months or even years down the line, when Barb is all but forgotten, those few remaining posters still pasted to telegraph poles are even farther removed from the original. They're now waterlogged and tattered. The girl in the photo is dead. The posters act as a folkloric memory of someone who once was but may no longer be. The Barbness of Barb, according to the poster, is a chilling reminder that sometimes people don't come home. Barb is no longer the beaming girl in the photo, nor is she the visual identifiers of the missing girl on the poster. She's dead and seemingly forgotten. The succession of models is identifiable to us as a process of endless Xeroxes or tape trade dubs. And with each step away from the original, the meaning is altered or lost.

The idea of hyperreality is less about a malicious intent to distort the world. It's more a matter of the passage of time and events. Much like our growth from child to adult, when we peel away those safety layers to reveal the complexities of the world, our surroundings wobble so much that whatever was there in the first place might not even be relevant now, let alone be decipherable.

Baudrillard cites Disneyland as an example. With its colorful characters and happiness *ad nauseum*, it captures the essence of childhood dreams. We know that unlike the outside world, Disneyland isn't real, but it reflects the cultural ideals of America: smiles, prosperity, and perfectly trimmed grass. Comfort is found here. As a result, the concept of the American dream, present for generations and instilled since birth, exists, but not as you might imagine it. The dream has been realized in Disneyland, but only in as much as it's a purchasable commodity. Your experience is timebound and proportionate to both money and imagination.

Baudrillard also points to reality television as a hyperreality. As far back as the 1970s we filmed everyday families leading seemingly normal lives to fulfill our own voyeuristic curiosities. The problem, however, is that the families know. There are cameras present. There is an audience. Any semblance of the everyday is stripped away because the situation is unique. If an argument occurs and the cameras are rolling, where does reality end and acting begin?

Let's not forget that in 1983, the US president was an actor famed for playing All-American heroes. Voters grew up watching those old black and white movies, and so did their kids. Like it or not, in the minds of many, Reagan was already a man who *could*. They'd seen him save the day a hundred times before. How would this time be any different? All of this makes for a very confusing time. Distinctions blur and life ceases to be straightforward when we acknowledge that the constructs of our cultural fabric aren't as stable as we thought—teenager and adult alike.

## It's Like Old Memories in the Back of My Head Only They're Not My Memories

As if life isn't difficult enough, the kids in *Stranger Things* have the added problem of all that supernatural stuff. They occupy a liminal space between two realities: the town of Hawkins and the Upside Down, a shadowy place that defies worldly logic. As the narrative unfolds the party's understanding of reality is weakened and altered by supernatural events. The fabric of reality is torn and the claw marks are deep in the belly of Hawkins. Alongside hyperreality and the whole teenage thing, they've now got the added mindfuck of monsters and murky flip-worlds. Even the laws of physics are thrown into question. The world was confusing before, but now it's brimming with abstract evil.

After the trick-or-treating incident in Season Two, Will is momentarily transported to the Upside Down and subjected to terrifying visions of the Mindflayer. Recuperating at home afterwards, he and Mike question whether their experiences are real. After all, Will is heavily medicated and Hawkins Lab has explained away all the weird stuff, so they *could* have imagined it. Deep down, the boys know that they're not losing their minds, even if they're afraid to admit it at first. In a moment of solidarity, Mike says to Will "If we both go crazy we'll go crazy together, right?"

For Mike, Will, and the other members of the Party, not only has the sense of reality shifted in the usual adolescent ways, it has sped into overdrive and blasted them through the planetary ceiling. There's now a spooky dark other-world, a strange plant-faced monster thing, and a monosyllabic mind-mage who flings trucks with her nosebleeds. That's a lot to process. All of these abnormalities culminate in a sense of shattered reality. They don't know what to believe anymore, and nor should they. Everything they used to believe has now been jeopardized by adults, by puberty, by society, and by the supernatural. Nobody will believe a word they say because their experiences are extraordinary. To the rest of the world they'd be liars, fantasists or mentally unwell. People already call Will a freak. All they have to rely on is each other.

The idea of the hyperreality trickles through the gaps in the pre-weirdness world of Hawkins in relatable ways. We might understand mass hallucinations and cultural agreements as a normative function of societies, whether they exist through intended enforcement, or simply because these pre-existing ideas and customs are thrust upon us from birth. The function of hyperreality probably isn't misleading by intent (lest aliens, lizard people, or the illuminati are real), but rather we understand the world in simplified or misunderstood ways because we don't have all the answers, we're not all experts in every field of study ever, and history has shaped us subconsciously in ways that are deeply engrained in culture. However, we don't have the complications of the Upside Down.

## It's Called Code Shut Your Mouth

As kids we used secret codes. We deflected mom's gaze from hickeys and hiccups with hand gestures and double-meanings.

In "Holly, Jolly," when Mike and El are hiding in the blanket fort, El reveals the danger she's in by saying "bad" and pressing two pointed fingers to her head. Much like Mike, we understand that this represents a gun. By pressing her fingers to her head, El is communicating danger, threat, and violence. What we acknowledge in the gesture isn't the physical pressing of finger to head, but the symbolism it communicates. We understand the gunfinger semiotically.

At its most basic, semiotics is the study of symbols. We're looking at the symbolic value that things hold rather than just the actual thing as it's presented. For Baudrillard, the world took a symbolic turn somewhere along the way. We lost reality because we're smothered with representation and interpretation. This isn't a linguistic thing. Rather than the whole thought-to-word ratio, Baudrillard linked the world to the fabric of culture.

We can see semiotics at work everywhere, even in the things we take for granted. It is in these things that we find the clearest examples. When you see a stop sign you know that you must stop because there is a risk of danger if you continue. It's a convention of culture that has existed for at least as long as we have had powered vehicles, or hidden cliffs, or any number of other risks. We also know that in the west, nodding your head means "Yes." It's a cultural custom that has existed for centuries. Yet, should you go to Iran, or Turkey, or any number of other countries, nodding would have the opposite implication and you could find yourself in a great confused mess, all because of one simple misunderstood gesture.

The idea of meaning being made in symbolic gestures is deeply engrained in human culture and we find semiotic value in even the most basic of human interactions. They are a nonverbal method of meaning making and communication and have probably existed long before the development of the spoken word. Symbols also extend to modern modes and developments within culture. We find symbols everywhere, and in the logocentric world of the 1980s, symbolism was rife.

Case in point: When you see the golden arches you know it means McDonald's and therefore fast food and burgers. It might equally mean, McNugget, America, evil corporation, unsettling clown, or any number of other things. Some of these things are mutually agreed (we can't deny the existence of the McNugget), whilst others are subjective (unsettling clown, I am looking at you).

Remember those ideas of Reagan representing the good old American hero? They are all semiotic interpretations found within Reaganism. Sure, you might not agree with them, but thousands did. That's why he was president. Now we're not here to discuss symbolism itself, so let's get to the meat of this. It's not about the symbolism *we* find in *Stranger Things*. It's about the signs and symbols our protagonists use to make sense of the whole abstract hyperreality.

Remember that the 1980s was subjected to the Satanic panic; Chick tracts warned of the dangers of Dungeons & Dragons. Just a year before the events of *Stranger Things*, the mania was further escalated by a young Tom Hanks in the terribad television movie, *Mazes and Monsters*. Parents everywhere feared that a twenty-sided die and copy of the *Dungeon Master's Guide* would turn their kids into horn-throwing glue sniffers.

In the pre-supernatural world of *Stranger Things*, D&D was little more than a simple pastime for the Party, but when Will disappeared and the monsters arrived the Satan thing suddenly became plausible. To Mike, Lucas, Dustin, and Will, the concepts found within D&D capture the horrors of the Upside Down. It's as close as they've ever come to the supernatural and even the game itself is make believe, it relates to their current experiences: there are good things and evil things, and the evil things are otherworldly and mysterious. Using Dungeons & Dragons as a frame of reference for all the weird spooky happenings is therefore both convenient and logical. Through D&D, the gang develop a type of meaning making.

Even El gets in on the act, swiping miniatures from the game board and flipping it over to explain the Upside Down. When the Party name the Demogorgon they do so not because the miniature physically resembles the flower-faced beast, but because its mythical counterpart evokes ideas of evil, other-worldliness, or even final boss. In the lore of Dungeons & Dragons it is the prince of demons.

By the end of Season Two, the party are so engrossed in D&D terminology that they even use it with outsiders, in this case Max and Hopper. Dustin declares it *"the best metaphor"* for what is going on (Lucas corrects this to "analogy"), and within the context of the Party he's right. It's not one hundred percent accurate, but it's quick and effective, and for the most part it works. In the hyperreal space they inhabit, D&D becomes a mutual mode of communication that fits the abstract nature of the Upside Down. (We shall overlook the fact that the Cthulhu mythos might have been more appropriate.)

## Friends Don't Lie

In "The Weirdo on Maple Street," Mike introduces El to the concepts of friendship and promise when he tells her "Promise, it means something that you can't break, ever." It's new to El because she's been a lab rat most of her life. Mike's instalove aside, trust develops gradually between the party and El, but Lucas is skeptical. El might be the monster.

But as El saves the boys with pant-pee/arm-break/van throwing, a mutual respect develops and once they've overcome Lucas's concerns, the Party accepts El as their newest member. They each understand that they're in this crazy mess together, even the icky girl with superpowers. But this only accounts for the Party and Eleven. Given that most of their interactions with adults since Will's disappearance are negative, it's understandable why they wouldn't want to share this with anyone else.

When Mike tells El that "friends . . . they tell each other things, things that parents don't know" it solidifies this whole teenage experience thing about codes. Coupled with El's experience of adults mostly as nefarious science goons, we understand why she's wary of adults too. We also know that through Hopper and Joyce, this mistrust of adults eventually changes, and it's one simple gesture from an adult to an adolescent that evidences the bold claim I made in the introduction.

## My Mom Will Get You Your Own Bed. You Can Eat as Many Eggos as You Want

By now you're wondering how Eggos fit into this. You want to know how Eggos will save the world and what makes them the true hero. To answer this we must return to the beginning.

Given that El has spent most of her life confined to Hawkins Lab, it's unlikely that she had control over what she ate. Whilst Eggos aren't the first thing she eats upon escape (that honor goes to the fries at Benny's diner), they're the first food we see her truly excited about. Hidden in the Wheeler household, Mike gives El her first taste of Eggos. She has never tasted anything so good before. We see the seeds of trust and friendship sown with golden crumbs of waffle. Unlike the Hawkins goons, the Party become Eleven's friends. They care for her. Some of them even want to kiss her, and she feels the same. And because of this Eggos take on a whole symbolic value that wouldn't exist otherwise.

Later, El steals Eggos from a local supermarket. As the narrative progresses we see El's love of Eggos increase exponentially to high levels of addiction. El's initial attachment stems from *enjoyment*. Eggos are an affirmation of positivity because she is free and they are a flavor found within that freedom. They connect with her on an intrinsic level because they make her feel good. That personal enjoyment, all those sugar rushes and new tastes, they go hand-in-hand with the other feelings that develop between her and the gang. By "The Upside Down," El is a true member of the Party. She has become their mage. The bond between the party members has strengthened as they've learned to trust each other, and Eggos have been present the whole time.

In the Season One finale when the party are holed up in Hawkins Middle School, Mike makes a promise to El, that once the whole supernatural mess is over, she can live with him and have as many Eggos as she wants. Shortly thereafter El warps the Demogorgon out of existence. She disappears with it, leaving only dust behind. Her absence is felt, most of all by Mike who begins his transformation into Emo Mike. And we're all empty too. After the roller-coaster of Season One we don't want to lose El. We're invested now. But then we see a glimmer of hope so powerful that we know everything will be all right in the end.

As Hawkins's future becomes increasingly uncertain, Eggos remain a constant. Much like the representations found in D&D, Eggos embody something greater than their simple surface value. Eggos become the glue that binds the party. Eggos are a gift, a commodity for exchange that says "I trust you." By locating *something* personal in Eggos, the gang has already transcended whatever meaning they held in the past: the simple snack is gone, instead imbued with the meaning Eleven and the gang have now created.

Any semiotic value that Eggos held prior to the onset of the weirdness, or outside of the gang's interactions, is now redundant. Much like the distortion we saw in the posters of Barb, Eggos are now several steps away from their original intent, but for the gang they communicate something much different and more powerful. As the layers of the hyperreality onion are further peeled, the value located within Eggos solidifies and intensifies to a degree that their impact transcends the direct communication between El and the gang and outwards towards others who are involved in the strange happenings.

So when soon-to-be-surrogate-grump-dad-Hopper skips out on the office Christmas party to place Eggos in that snow covered box, El knows that she can trust him. That egg-batter gift is so much more than tasty goodness; Eggos are a beacon. In all that darkness and uncertainty they bring the Party together and anchor the foundations of hope and friendship. They even guide the missing back to the fold, and when the missing are capable of kicking the butts of all supernatural evils, then you know you've found a winner.

## Nobody Normal Ever Accomplished Anything Meaningful in This World

Before you tell me that you feel cheated and that Eggos aren't really the hero—they're not even sentient, let alone psionic—they have played a larger part in the salvation of Hawkins than you cared to admit. You knew all along that El would be back because you too saw Hopper stash those Eggos in the woods. You let the fear of no return wash over you as you waited anxiously between seasons, but deep down you knew. And herein lies the greatest power of Eggos: the trust and friendship the Party locates within Eggos extends beyond the screen to you, the viewer.

All of those feels, those heart-thumps, and swoons, they're not just the product of great scripting and performances. Instead, through Eggos you've participated in this world of *Stranger Things*, because the hands of friendship and trust have been extended to you. The distinction between the fictional world of *Stranger Things* and the world you inhabit has become blurred, and maybe, just maybe, hyperreality isn't the dumb abstract of an idea it first seemed.

In a world that no longer makes sense, salvation is found in a microwavable egg-batter breakfast snack. They are Hawkins's greatest hope not because of any obvious outward power but for the semiotic values they hold.

# 9
# To Err Is Human, to Forget . . . Sublime

CHERISE HUNTINGFORD

> I've come to the conclusion that most of the things that we remember about our childhood are lies.
>
> —STEPHEN KING, *It*

Stephen King's book *It*—possibly the heftiest influence on *Stranger Things*—ends with a barely pubescent sewer sex scene. One girl, six boys . . . it's a Dark Web screenshot in a Delorean; thrust back four decades to when technicolor was still drying on our TV sets, and Pac-Man ruled adolescence.

The final pages of the author's second longest tome are crust-thick with absurdity; and yet, somewhere in the fetid labyrinth of the Derry waterworks, the sensory impressions of The First Time are captured with regrettable clarity: the metallic tang, a damp discomfort, and the prescience that a compact lifetime of childhood is about to be despoiled without ceremony.

In another universe—small town Hawkins—Season One of *Stranger Things* wraps up in typical sci-fi bombast, with Eleven being sacrificially sucked into an extra-terrestrial void. The Demogorgon is dead. The boyfriends are saved—chastity intact. And El, resurrected by the will of a sentimental audience, survives; saved by the burly-but-tender-hearted trope of a sheriff and the sustaining magic of Eggos.

*It* is the banal ruin of innocence; the epitaph that growing up *fucks up* childhood. The Biblical caveat that knowledge is death . . . so it's better to forget. Worlds away from King's words, *Stranger Things* is the antidote: the fugue state in which we can dispense with Truth—and memory; a machination of false nostalgia to rescue us from what's real. But are these alternate dimensions mutually exclusive? Or do we tightrope the space between our gilded construction of reality and the subconscious shadows of our Upside Down? And is the lie preferable because it just feels better—or is its flaw of optimism an essential evil?

## Now Memories . . . Or Never Memories?

We are homesick most for the places we have never known.

—CARSON MCCULLERS

Kiddy-eating killer clown aside—*It,* the story of a group of dorky pre-teens uncovering a subterranean, malevolent alien entity, is the ostensible blueprint for *Stranger Things*. At its core, however, Stephen King's book is less about sci-fi scares than it is a study of the cerebral otherness of childhood; more specifically the power and potency of childhood memory.

The Duffer Brothers handle this theme differently. It's not a distinct part of the plot, but a device readily exploited via their show's 1980s setting—a decade when most of us watching would've been kids ourselves. *Stranger Things* reframes childhood in the Eighties via a storyline that inverts one of the seminal works which inspired it.

It encourages us to remember—*or at least think we remember*—its hair-scrunchies-and-synth-pop mise-en-scène, asphyxiating its King-esque plot in the distilled neon goo of Eighties pop culture—a falsified nostalgia for a time that only ever existed on screen. It's a shared myth in which *Stranger Things* allows viewers to indulge, and the supernatural stuff that happens makes an easy allegory for the fact that our memories of times gone by are vulnerable to incredible creative license.

Nostalgia is a heady thing; psychotropic, it can distort perceptions of the past and render memories a masterpiece of rosy-painted fiction. From the outset, *Stranger Things* presents a sentimentalized picture of that usually fragile precipice overlooking pubescence. Of course, there's the stereotypical gang of big-talk bullies, the attending awkwardness of a crush, and the angst of being parentally misunderstood (sans the solace of Snapchat), yet it all works towards crystallizing that epoch as ultimately endearing. In this case, youth equates to essential goodness, and something like goodness prevails. Even when the world itself is under threat of *Aliens*-style invasion, the kids of Hawkins have their walking Deus Ex Machina BFF to put things right; unlike the Losers Club in *It, their* childhood isn't quite as screwed: Eleven claws her way out of ectoplasm and certain death, and the boys live to play another day at Dungeons & Dragons. It's fantasy, of course. It's bullshit, too.

*It,* as is King's way, is a dissimilar beast.

In the make-believe 'burb of Derry, a hotspot for the paranormal and the degenerate, a group of unpopular preteens stumble upon a nightmare in the municipal sewer systems. The Dancing Clown, Pennywise, or, more famously, *It,* is emblematic of what children fear: a distortion of the norm, the unpredictability of the commonplace. *It* is metaphor, of course; an examination of horror in the home—absence, abuse, neglect, and loss. And the clown as evil being is just a glyph. His talent for shapeshifting into the individual, primordial fear of each member of the Losers Club is more a descriptor of the power of imagination as the final vestige of youth, reaching its climax at the pivotal point where the disenchantment of adulthood looms. The protagonists ultimately defeat *It* by doing away with the childish chimera, confronting its unadorned, gruesome essence, but the cost is high, and not everyone escapes the drainpipe catacombs intact.

An anthology of all-too-real domestic traumas only amplified by the presence of a polymorphous monster, the tone of the book is discomfiting, despairing—the crux being that life for a child is perhaps best not remembered. For many of us, this was the Reagan era, all right; but not the one we're loading up on memory lane merch to relive.

Thus, as adults, we forget; and so we have to recreate—or *create*—in our heads, a happier moment in time. Enter Eleven and the gang, a Hanna-Barbera tableau with an edge . . . and a safety catch.

*Cherise Huntingford*

# When My Gifts Were Strong Enough, I Used Them to Escape

It is singular how soon we lose the impression of what ceases to be constantly before us. A year impairs, a luster obliterates. There is little distinct left without an effort of memory, then indeed the lights are rekindled for a moment—but who can be sure that the Imagination is not the torch-bearer?

—LORD BYRON

Mnemosyne, the Titan queen of memory, was also the goddess of wisdom, and the mother of Clio, goddess of history. The genealogy is no coincidence. Ancient Greek philosophers believed history and wisdom to be the direct products of the art of memory: for history to *exist*, we must conjure it through remembering; and memories themselves were seen as the prerequisite to human thought—to consciousness itself. Our proof of existence.

But the Greek etymology of the word 'nostalgia', a fond recollection of the past, in common parlance, together with its later coinage as a pathological term for the longing for a place impossible to reach—and then, scientific research into the unreliability of memory—throws a curveball at this Classical insistence on mnemonic power.

The ancient Greek word *nostimon* is the etymon, or forebear, of nostalgia. It first appears in Homer's *Odyssey*, to describe how Odysseus, long separated from home and love, yearns for his "day of return"—or *nostimon emar*. The poem chronicles ten years of swashbuckling mythical beasts, communing with Olympian deities, and the righteous vengeance that only imagination can offer. The homesick hero eventually returns to halcyon days; but you don't need to read the tale to know that Troy isn't quite how he left it.

The Odyssey is shades of the Hawkins squad's fantastical adventures, knuckling up against netherworld denizens (and freshman bullies), utilizing El's transdimensional talent to help them on their way. But it's the darker Derry—*It*'s lair—where Homer's ultimate moral lies: The Losers Club, now grown, must return to the *truth* of their childhood—not some Trojan fantasy—after having exiled themselves from the memory.

More than a millennium after the Greco-Roman collapse, *nostalgia* is born. Coined by Swiss physician Johannes Hofer in 1688, nostalgia shifts from diasporic emotion to disease—thought to be "triggered by excessive exposure to foreign environments." Hofer studies Swiss mercenaries who are shipped off to engage in the horror of war. He observes such manic-depressive symptoms as loss of appetite, a heightened suicide rate, and having visions of yearned for people and places. Among the soldiers nostalgia runs rampant—playing "Khue-Reyen," an old Swiss milking song (that reportedly sends men into fits of agonizing reminiscence), will get you executed. As virulent and persistent as the Black Death, nostalgia crosses long-fortified borders; in 1790, desperate French doctor Jourdan Le Cointe threatens those afflicted with a jab from a "red-hot poker." A more economic Russian general buries alive any showing the dreaded nostalgic symptoms·

Even today, we continue to misunderstand the nostalgia phenomenon, attaching too much credence to the memories it selectively beckons for our mollifying benefit. It's not the substance, but the act itself that is significant—nostalgia is neither illness nor a fond recollection of the past, but an *escape*. "The nostalgic," Susan Stewart writes in *On Longing: Narratives of the Miniature, the Gigantic, the Souvenir, the Collection*, "is enamored of distance, not of the referent itself."

The soldiers didn't wish to be home so much as they wished to be transported from imminent death. Home was merely a vanishing point on which to cling—a cipher as insubstantial as gunsmoke. In the same way, Hawkins, a fictional mark on a made-up map, is just a template for escape. The *Frankenstein*-ish science-experiment-gone-bad is a hook, sure, but it's the nostalgic pull away from our present selves that reels us in; the rewind of that greatest hits mixtape that keeps us hitting play—and *Stranger Things* lets us play at being young, dumb, and immortal again; if only one episode at a time.

Literary critic Linda Hutcheon summarizes the appealing lie of nostalgia in poetic frankness: it "exiles us from the present as it brings the imagined past near." One group of thinkers, the Romantics, saw looking back to the past for what it was. They drew away from realism—the dread of Blake's "dark satanic mills"—trading it in for an alternate reality, saturated in sentiment for a simpler time, uncomplicated by the industrialized, turbulent discontent of their era.

The relationship between Romanticism and nostalgia is so frequently cited, that today, the two are almost synonymous. And the thread between is the summoning and sculpting of memories, to create an aesthetically pleasing, although melancholic, tribute to what is now—or has always been—out of reach. *Stranger Things*, along with so many 1980s-set, John Hughes homages, taps into this Romantic tendency; romanticized to the point where the decade references a series of wistful, culturally-bound childhood emblems, not an actual, objective moment in history. What results is something transcendent of fact; and more powerful in its effect.

The Romantics acknowledged that nostalgia had this sort of power, but not in the same way the ancient philosophers perceived. Although Romantics were influenced by philosophies of antiquity, they diverged from the Greeks' functional, idealised perspective: the past was inspiration, not to be relied upon as record, but a palette upon which to layer a utopian nostalgia. In this, they also opposed Dr. Hofer's pathological cast on nostalgic longing: to yearn could be beautiful; sublime, even. Yet tellingly, they still acknowledged the inherent irrationalism of the exercise. This was the eternal struggle infusing the work of every artist, poet, and creator of the time: to long for that which never was.

## Is This All Real? Or Is It Like the Doctors Say, All in Your Head?

It is an illusion that youth is happy, an illusion of those who have lost it.

—W. Somerset Maugham

*Stranger Things* is legit sci-fi fantasy fiction—it's not expected to be anything less, or any more refined.

In the context of genre, our suspension of disbelief is both presumed and required. We enter into the contract knowingly to chew and swallow up notions of monsters and superhumans. And a motley crew of misfits destined to kick evil ass.

But there's the small print nobody reads.

*Stranger Things* ratchets up its popularity not so much through its actual story, but in its manipulation of memory. It's a montage of everything you ever loved as a Generation X-er growing up, or what you're *pretty* sure you remember loving. When a show revels in retro reference, it can plug up the amnesiac gaps in our past via *vicarious nostalgia*—that feeling of yearning for a moment which, while occurring outside the span of your memory, is (as Gilad Padva puts it), "relatable and has sentimental value *due to repeated mediated exposure to it.*"

In Hawkins, we relive our simulated youth not just as voyeur of Nancy's depressing mom jeans or lipsynching to Toto's *Africa*; but in the very atmosphere of the place—that earnest thrill of being a child in the days before smart phones, online porn, and helicopter parenting. And when terrorism was only an underground Soviet threat, effused with the distant quality of a spy film on a 2D screen.

Admittedly, of the bona fide 1980s decade, and to quote Spandau Ballet, this much is (or was) true. But it's not the whole story, and the rest of what *Stranger Things* would have you believe was the Eighties *you* lived through, is cribbed straight from celluloid.

American novelist Kurt Andersen explains the circular creative process inspired by (and perpetuating) vicarious nostalgia. Screenwriters

> usually retain a sense of emotional connection to the media of their childhood and, in turn, will create art that is either consciously or unconsciously informed by what resonated with them when they were growing up. ("You Say You Want a Devolution?")

The provenance of nostalgic art is not anything more profound or distinct than nostalgic art itself.

The Duffer team resurrect the decade using TV and movie tropes so deeply ingrained in our consciousness that they've merged imperceptibly with our individual histories. They are no longer recognized as deliberate narrative devices; they have become simply, primordially evocative and we respond as reflex. And our lizard brain can't tell if our childhood was an uncanny replica of Mike, Dustin, Lucas.

and Will's—if being a kid had us freewheeling down suburbia *en route* to the arcade and endless possibilities . . . or nothing like it at all.

Advertisers admit to toying with the constructive nature of memory; instead of cuing actual past experiences, a carefully crafted ad that implies a cosy nostalgia can change autobiographical memory—supplanting what happened with what the scene says happened. Take Stewart's Root Beer, for example. The brand reports many adults remembering growing up drinking their frosty root beer in those signature dark glass bottles—impossible, since the company only began distributing full-scale a short ten years ago. Before that, they were just a fountain beverage.

Elizabeth Loftus has discussed the way in which one notorious study involving the sentimental power of Disney illustrates that sentimentality can be entirely contrived in the absence of any authentic experience. Participants were certain that as children they'd shaken hands with an impossible character at the theme park—non-Disney Bugs Bunny—because they'd been exposed to nostalgic ads convincing them of this. This delusion, along with misremembering Stewart's Root Beer points to a major security breach in cognition: memory's unregulated malleability.

The reconstruction happens in any medium—most powerfully in the intensive setting of cinema and Netflix binges. *Stranger Things* does it with the loud-mouthed swagger of a day-glo tracksuit, and we're blind to the trick. In fact, *Stranger Things* goes one step further than movie pastiche and subverts the familiar Eighties tropes themselves to fit in with our present-day thin-skinned milieu.

In Season Two, jerk jock Steve is redeemed into an endearing dad stand-in for the younger boys, swapping out his original 1980s teen-movie stereotype for something we can feel fuzzier about. And throughout the series, protagonist Will is vaguely coded as homosexual, but the persecution theme of his story arc has nothing to do with this—he's just in the wrong place at the wrong time. If this were the *real* 1980s, stricken with AIDS panic, it is unlikely that the character would have been in the series at all. The show breeds nostalgia for a time that didn't exist off-screen, and not quite on it, either.

Beyond the deliberate, zeitgeist-charged anachronisms—and the fact that that plot-defining Demogorgon figurine in the Wheeler's basement never actually existed in 1983—it's the underlying fairy story of what it was like to be young (in the 1980s or whenever), a Rousseauian ideal of unblemished childhood, that messes with our own memories the most. Probably unwittingly, this twist of truth is encapsulated by the following vignette.

In an effort to make Will feel better about his oneiric Up-side-Down terrors, jolly, doomed-to-die Bob recounts child-hood coulrophobic nightmare, Mr Baldo: "Hey kiddo, would you like a balloon?"("The Pollywog")—the hammy reference to *It*'s monster-clown is delivered with a smirk; a comical aside that denies the real fear factor of its predecessor, saying, *we're only playing here, folks*.

King, of course, doesn't play. His tour-de-force *It* carries weight not just because it's 1,138 pages long, but because it's full of the bloated heaviness of reality. A gritty mimeograph of the 1980s in a nowhere burg where sometimes, children turn up dead, and the miscreations of science fiction are a paper cut compared to what waits for you at home.

In *Stranger Things* the monster is fantasy inserted into reality—with just as fantastical, supernatural counterpowers with which to defend. The monster is straight up metaphor in *It*: the memories of our childhood that are too much to bear. The only salve to no longer remember. And, to be clear, hard-core trauma is nonessential in our desire to forget—the simple banality of loneliness, so quintessential to any and every child is enough to wish ourselves anywhere but here. The mechanism for nostalgic projection is already nascent in our earliest days—ripe imagination, and a fecund mind.

## Nothing Is Gonna Go Back to the Way that It Was. Not Really

Memory goes wrong in mundane and minor, or in dramatic and disastrous ways.

—JOHN SUTTON, "Memory"

The Mind Flayers are a race of monstrous beings hailing from an unknown D&D dimension, using psionic powers to enslave and control others. One of them shows up in Season Two of *Stranger Things*, only *inside* of Will Byers. The ex-abductee, already primed for exploitation, is possessed by the creature, which intermittently uses Will's baby-face facade to trick and trap those around him.

The Mind Flayer is not an intentional reference to memory; but it's no stretch to infer the diabolical nature of the powers of recollection—Will talks of "now memories," a kind of prescience that ends up being sometimes true, and sometimes a ruse to round up folks like a Demogorgon ready meal. Although Will is 'Will the Wise' in the boys' basement fort, in real life he's a captive of some malevolent force and we can't trust his control over his own mind.

While *It* digs down into the grittiness of things that happen, and *Stranger Things* functions as a nostalgic *escape from* the things that happen, *both* use their fantasy elements allegorically. For example, as "The Mind Flayer" episode reaches its climax, the beasts of the Upside Down claw their way through the rift torn open by El's psychokinesis, converging on Hawkins's Lab, a Freudian terror of confronting all the hidden and forgotten shit (its sole aim, destruction).

At the same time, the show touches on memory distortion more directly (for all *Stranger Things*'s differences with *It*, inventing memories is in our DNA; it can't help but come out in any and every human story)—when Joyce Byers asks police chief Hopper to help her find her missing son, relaying the impossible events surrounding his disappearance, Hopper's response is poignant. He tells her that after his daughter's death, he thought he saw her and heard her, too. He had to accept those seemingly paranormal visitations for his grieving mind playing tricks on him: "Otherwise, I was going to fall down a hole, that I couldn't get out of" ("The Body"). His words aren't just a macabre reference to how Hopper believes Will has died, but *An Alice in Wonderland* allusion to going down the rabbit hole of insanity; for misinterpreting events and committing them to sacred memory.

This idea is augmented by Joyce's dreams, woven in with flashbacks of Will; her nocturnal recollections have a veil of non-reality as she visits Will in his makeshift fort, Castle Byers, their encounter shot through with shafts of celestial light and too-bright color—that rosy retrospection ("The Vanishing of Will Byers").

In the second installment of *Stranger Things* Will is afflicted with the *anniversary effect,* a real psychological phenomenon that, around the anniversary of a traumatic event, confronts the sufferer with an unusually high number of memories of their trauma. The mechanism behind this may be evolutionary—a kind of protective reminder not to repeat past mistakes, but more simply, it's also down to our emotional brainstem being unable to perceive time; a telltale reminder of pain is enough to send you hurtling back into that moment of agony, now made verbose and less true to the original event with the warping of years. The anniversary of Will's abduction coincides with Halloween; when the dead walk, necromanced *en masse* to terrify the living. This connection heightens the illusory, fantastical quality of memories resurfaced, culminating in El entering into her mother's private Hell of remembering only a loop of strung-together, seemingly meaningless snatches of misery: "Breathe, sunflower, rainbow, . . . 450" ("Dig Dug").

The problem is that we assume the act of remembering to be infallible; a Eucharistic rite delivered straight from Truth and transmuted into sensory facsimile of fact. But the brain is as sensitive to defect and damage as any organ, limb, or fingernail. If memory were indeed infallible, the recollection of childhood for many of us would be closer to King's, not the Duffer brothers', but ultimately, *Stranger Things* is about the business of fiction. Jim Hopper realizes he's misjudged Joyce. She isn't confused by grief: Will is alive and held prisoner by interdimensional terrorists. Her memory is untouchable . . . by the ravages of real life.

## I Tried to Make It Go Away. But It Got Me

A person's memory is everything, really. Memory is identity. It's you.

— STEPHEN KING

If the idea of false nostalgia is a misnomer—*nostalgia* is sufficient enough of a term in its inherent falseness—what does that mean for our sense of personal history?

If you had to take the nostalgic faux feelings effected by *Stranger Things*'s Tangerine Dream–ish soundtrack, teased hair, and BMXs for what they are—just another fantasy element to intensify the escapism, what does that imply for our nostalgia over things *not* on screen? What does that mean for the things rooted in the unique significance of each person's past?

Back in ancient Greece, Mnemosyne, the deity whose dominion included wisdom and remembrance; and whose child was history, was also mother to the nine muses (Clio, Euterpe, Thalia, Melpomene, Terpsichore, Erato, Polymnia, Ourania, and Calliope, each of whom has, as legends claim, served as a source of artistic inspiration). There was the idea that memories are powerful motivators of creation.

Alissa Michelle Cook writes how the ethereal sisters "sing a song that conjures madness, and then when the madness fades, they flit from their hosts and slip into shadows, leaving the artist with hazy half-forgotten memories." And this is precisely how nostalgia works, mixing real experience with some figment from our fantasies. It's an entirely unconscious alchemy that nonetheless pervades our waking hours with near-overpowering feeling. A feeling so strong we don't doubt its veracity. It's Joyce and her stoicism, Will and his now memories—and those sentimental feels you get watching Mike and the crew indulge in innocence within their basement fort.

Philosopher and psychiatrist Neel Burton describes nostalgia as "a form of self-deception in that it invariably involves distortion and idealization of the past, not least because the bad or boring bits fade from memory more quickly than the peak experiences." Burton warns that an overindulgence in our innate nostalgic tendencies can create a false autobiography, a pretend past that has the capacity to ultimately distort our perception of self.

Others in the field of memory study extend the function of nostalgia into something deliberately existential: *to overcome feelings of meaninglessness*. In this way, and to echo Burton's caveat, memories are more about wish fulfillment, summoned muses of the self-narrative. In *Stranger Things*, we're transported to a moment in which life was unchartered and where shitty decisions are light years away . . . we could still be something, somebody, someday.

Let's not forget that the 1980s fictional template is interchangeable with any decade; there's nothing especially unique to the time—the prerequisites are only that it conjures freedom and fantasy . . . and some recognizable artefacts to both trigger and muddy the memory. (Even El's signature Eggos can wield this effect; in 2016, breakfast giant Kellogg's offered a replica print-out of their Eggo's Waffle box from 1983, for fans to create *Stranger Things* Halloween get-ups. It was a pretty banal prop, outside of its filmic connection, but its apparent ties to our youth make it something of an irresistible time-travel talisman. It's also little surprise that Eggos sales enjoy a significant boost with the airing of *Stranger Things*.)

The comfort of nostalgia is captured via the French adage *"plus ça change, plus c'est la même chose,"* an expression used to convey the unchanging essence of things, in spite of social and technological advancement. As Kurt Anderson explains, now "that saying has acquired an alternative and nearly opposite definition: the more *certain* things change for real (technology, the global political economy), the more *other* things (style, culture) stay the same."

Nostalgia's function is to moor ourselves to something the flux of time cannot erode: our memories. Which is an exercise in irony—something King builds into the very structure of *It*. The way the novel is written, *It* is a melding of timelines, weaving the past and present in and out of each other, cutting more rapidly between the two until they juxtapose almost imperceptibly—like stopping mid-sentence in 1958 and picking up with the end of the sentence in 1985.

One especially memorable time-funk occurs on an almost esoteric level: as adults, the Losers Club share a scar on their hands, a reminder of their blood pact to return to Derry and kill the clown—when they do come back to their past and defeat Pennywise, the scars have disappeared; the moment is erased. This stylistic maneuver isn't just about keeping a lengthy book dynamic; it depicts how memories, when called into conscious recollection, are altered by the very act of remembering. (In stark contrast, the static time capsule of *Stranger Things*—where there is no chronological hopscotch, only dreams—is our escape hatch from this unreliable, unnerving fluidity.)

On the grander, collective scale of history, which is essentially a composition of what our ancestors have remembered from their experiences and selectively recorded, is as amendable as our own private recollections; "subject to the dominant fervor of any one particular time," and ready to metamorphose according to what narrative best suits the current agenda.

John Locke believed in this persuasive pull of memory, asserting remembering, knowledge, and history to be products of consciousness—and consciousness itself to be shaped by the very same triptych. In this way, Locke affirms the Greek synthesis of mnemonics and the self-concept, but he goes further, and beyond the Romantics' artistic acquisition of memory and its distortion—to how forgetting can make us lose sight of our very identity.

In his 1690 book, *An Essay concerning Human Understanding*, Locke suggests that the self is "a thinking intelligent being, that has reason and reflection, and can consider itself as itself, the same thinking thing, in different times and places" and defines personal identity succinctly as "the sameness of a rational being." In other words, he proposes that your personal identity is an expression of your consciousness. And memory, a central element in consciousness, is therefore a necessary condition of personal identity: "as far as consciousness can be extended backwards to any past action or thought, so far reaches the identity of that person; it is the same self now as it was then."

So how do we reconcile our impressionable memory with maintaining identity? We don't. When it comes to forgetting, or misremembering, Locke claims that, "in all these cases, our consciousness being interrupted, and we losing sight of our past selves, doubts are raised whether we are the same thinking thing."

Critics of Locke's *Essay* attempt to refine his view of identity's construction, claiming that memory is not a prerequisite for a solid identity but rather one form of evidence for the continuity of consciousness, and thus continued identity. And yet, people struck with severe forms of amnesia typically also lose their identity nearly altogether—as detailed by late writer and neurologist Oliver Sacks in his case study of forty-nine-year-old Jimmy G, the "lost mariner," who struggles to find meaning as he can't recall anything after his late adolescence. (Will's memory loss via Mind Flayer hints at this potential catastrophe, too.)

Locke's psychological continuity theory of personal identity comes full circle from its Classical origins—the likes of which were so certain of ontological import—to confound us with our own meaninglessness. Because we're human, and because our awareness of our humanity is constructed from human systems, the margin for error is exorbitant. Who needs demodogs, Mind Flayers, and the clown that eats kids when it's your own mind that can erase you? The denizens of fantasy *out there* only serve to switch your attention from the scariest thing *inside*: the dissolution of self once the phenomenon of *remembering* the self is broken down.

## There's Nothing for You Back There

One of the keys to happiness is a bad memory.

—Rita Mae Brown

Eleven revisits her past in Season Two of *Stranger Things* ("The Lost Sister"), and the brief departure from Hawkins seems out of place; a schizoid moment in the script. The heroine joins an emo band of miscreants that coerces her into retaliation acts (and a painfully punk-lite wardrobe). The dissonance is shared between viewer and character: piecing together facts from what came before proves unhelpful. If anything, it threatens what we love about El—her identity as the girl with only a vague backstory, an enigma almost supernatural; a bona fide comic-book superheroine.

Psychologist Giuliana Mazzoni asserts that not having *every* memory at our disposal is a good thing; and contorting what we do remember perhaps even better. Mazzoni explains that the self we recall from the past requires constant updating to preserve a "positive, up-to-date sense of self." Because, basically, we're human—the shorthand: we're weak, we're victims, we're aggressors, and we're shit. And constant confrontation with this truth would only be sufferable by sociopaths. So we fall back on nostalgia.

When *Stranger Things* ends with the Snow Ball—the prom cliché with the awkward First Kiss that's impossible not to be endearing—the tender moment is something like *déjà vu*. It's our happy place; a place so familiar . . . *we're pretty sure ours was just like it*. And then, in *It* even Stephen King succumbs to the salve of poor memory:

> He awakens from this dream unable to remember exactly what it was, or much at all beyond the simple fact that he has dreamed of being a child again. He touches his wife's smooth back as she sleeps her warm sleep and dreams her own dreams; he thinks it is good to be a child, but it is also good to be a grownup and able to consider the mystery of childhood . . .

Bill Denbrough, the unspoken leader of the Losers Club, emerges from what he thinks is a diaphanous dream, the edges quickly fading into abstraction in the way of all dreams. He has forgotten all that came before—*almost*; save for *a hazy, but not unpleasant, impression of childhood.*

We could lament the awful irony that you only appreciate the value of retrospect when you are old enough for time to have warped your recollection. That our childhoods are largely stories we curl up with at night. That our own children remember so little of these days—and what memories they do have will be subject to the distortion that comes with being human. Or we could just remember the 1980s however the hell we want to . . . it's our birthright as imaginative beings. (High waistbands? Never happened). The truth is we cannot survive some horrors, but we can live with a lie. It may not be what is real, or true.

But it's what we tune in for.

# IV

## How Strange
## Are We?

# 10
# Stranger Shadows

DANIEL CORNELL

In the beginning, . . . darkness was upon the face of the deep.

—Genesis

"Something is coming; something hungry for blood; a shadow grows on the wall behind you, swallowing you in darkness. *It* is almost here." These words are spoken by Mike Wheeler in the very first episode of *Stranger Things*, "The Vanishing of Will Byers." While spoken in the context of a seemingly innocuous game of Dungeons & Dragons, these words will prove undeniably portentous as the series unfolds.

The Demogorgon appears and Will Byers rolls a seven. "It got me." These words foreshadow his fate for much of the rest of the first two seasons. On his bike ride home the appearance of a monstrous silhouette in the middle of the road forces him down into a ditch. The spectral creature stalks through his yard, visible from the window at the back of his house. The light intensifies in his shed and then, in a blast of light, both Will and the monster disappear.

We can interpret the opening of the series and the first two seasons in terms of what the psychoanalyst Carl Gustav Jung called *the Shadow*. "But what *is* the Shadow?" you must surely ask. Jung introduced the idea of the shadow into analytic psychology and, in addition, it plays an important part in his philosophy of *the self*.

We talk about *ourselves* a lot, or we may tell someone to look after herself, and so on. We may think of the world as

being populated by numerous selves with there being a corre-
lation between selves and the physical bodies of humans that
inhabit the world. However, in both philosophy and psychology,
the self is often understood as the experiencing subject. Jung
understands the Shadow to be a key component of the self.

## The Mind and Self

Jung understands the self as composed of *at least two* distinct parts, namely the *conscious-ego* and the *unconscious
shadow*. Jung's model of the mind is, broadly speaking, comprised of the conscious ego (not to be confused with Eggos),
the unconscious shadow and their relationship to one another. It is their relationship to one another which constitutes the *self*.

## Ego-Consciousness

We may think of ourselves as individuals who interact with
the world, typically by means of our five senses, sight, touch,
taste, smell, and hearing, which also give us an awareness
of that world. Think of this awareness as our consciousness.
Think of the games Dragon's Lair and Dig Dug that Dustin
plays in the arcade.

While playing the games, Dustin is aware, or conscious,
of the sights and sounds of the game, the bright flashing onscreen visuals, the 8-bit soundtrack and the way the joystick
feels in his hand as he attempts to control the onscreen action. These are all an awareness of what is commonsensically
thought of as the *external* world or, more particularly, of objects in the external world. Before having done any philosophy we normally think that objects would continue to exist
if we were not there to be conscious of it.

Some people think that, for example, colors only exist in
the mind while physical objects such as tables, chairs, arcade
machines and so on exist independently of the mind. There
is a philosophical position called *naive* or *direct realism* that
holds that we see the world directly, unmediated by colors
existing in the mind. This is the common-sense view.

Dustin also feels frustration at losing his high score at
Dig Dug to Max. This frustration that Dustin feels, unlike

the objects perceived by our five senses is Dustin's mental state. We may think of this awareness of ourselves or this ability to reflect on our mental states as self-consciousness. Jung had a distinct concept of the self which is why he instead labeled this type of consciousness as *ego-consciousness*. This consciousness is directed towards our ego and not our selves. It is therefore, for Jung, Dustin's ego that experiences the world when he loses the high score.

# The Shadow

According to Jung,

> The shadow is a moral problem that challenges the whole ego-personality, for no one can become conscious of the shadow without considerable moral effort. To become conscious of it involves recognizing the dark aspects of the personality as present and real. This act is the essential condition for any kind of self-knowledge, and it therefore, as a rule, meets with considerable resistance. (*Aion*, p. 8)

The shadow cannot be considered in isolation any more than the ego can. We must also take heed of its relation to self-knowledge and the self, the latter of which, for Jung, represented the unity of the shadow and the ego. In order to achieve self-knowledge and self-mastery and no longer be a slave to the shadow, the unconscious and our primitive instincts, the shadow of the unconscious needs to be integrated with the conscious ego.

There are at least three things to consider about the shadow:

1. **The relationship between the shadow and the conscious ego.**

2. **The moral problem of the shadow, since it is construed as harboring those dark parts of the personality that we do not acknowledge.**

3. **The relationship between the shadow and self-knowledge.**

With regard to these three separate points above, 1. is present most in Season One, as seen in the way in which the

Upside Down begins to manifest itself in the everyday world of experience, while 2. is a theme that runs throughout the first two seasons, since Eleven's supernatural abilities always have an element of moral ambiguity to them, for example, when she kills other people to survive. 3. becomes more relevant in Season Two when, for example, El begins to understand her past and who she is.

Since the self is made up of the conscious ego and the unconscious shadow, to have knowledge or understanding of ourselves requires that we face up to the uglier aspects of our human nature that reside in the unconscious part of the mind.

There are, importantly, two manifestations of the shadow to consider. There is the shadow as *archetype* and the shadow as *that aspect of the self with which each individual must contend*. In the former case, Jung presented the shadow as being shared as part of the unconscious mind of all people. This is essentially what, in Jung's view, an archetype is. It's an element of the collective unconscious of humanity.

Just as we think of ourselves as sharing or partaking in the world with other people, the shadow is itself a kind of shared unconscious realm. In that sense it is part of our common humanity, perhaps like the DNA we share. In *Stranger Things*, this is represented as becoming conscious by the intrusion of the Upside Down and all its monsters into the everyday world of Hawkins.

Will also claims that his visions of the Shadow Monster as a dark, tentacled, gigantic creature are akin to staring pure evil in the face. He shares that vision with El. Both El and Will represent the incorporation, in various degrees, of the shadow into the personality. Both of these characters incorporate it in different ways.

In Will the shadow is presented as something dangerous which consumes him when he becomes possessed by the Shadow Monster. In Eleven's case, the incorporation can be seen to have a heroic aspect; she is capable of using her otherworldly powers to defeat the threats facing Hawkins and her friends.

## The Shadow in *Stranger Things*

What is the Upside Down? It looks like an underground world full of terrifying monsters and creatures. It also appears as organic and natural in contrast to the town of Hawkins. It bears a striking resemblance to certain mythic depictions of the Underworld, such as Hades in Greek mythology as well as holding some semblance to the Christian Hell. It's a hostile dimension which presents a profound, pervasive, and omnipresent existential threat on the flipside of the everyday world where the citizens of Hawkins live. We can think of the Upside Down as being an externalized manifestation of the shadow-side of the unconscious mind. It is a world filled with physical danger as well as mental anguish.

Season One contains the most in relation to the development of the shadow imagery insofar as it sets the stage for Season Two which then deals with the problem of self-knowledge and the related themes of the identity and development of the individual particularly with regards to El's character.

## The Moral Dimension of the Upside Down

In the show's first episode, perhaps talking hyperbolically, the worst thing to have apparently happened in Hawkins before Will's disappearance was, according to the Police Chief Jim Hopper "When an owl attacked Eleanor Gillespie's head because it thought her hair was a nest." It seems the writers' intentions with this comment is that we are to regard the town of Hawkins as having been some kind of haven, which certainly makes for a stark contrast with that of the Upside Down.

In "The Flea and The Acrobat," while Dustin reads from his book of Dungeons & Dragons lore, he describes the Upside Down as being "like the vale of shadows." He goes on, "The vale of shadows is a dimension that is a dark reflection or echo of our world. It is a place of decay and death: a place of monsters. It is right next to you and you don't even see it."

Clearly the opposites of decay, death, and monsters are growth, life and people—the kinds of things to which the people of Hawkins are accustomed. The Upside Down is both the literal opposite in terms of its location and its figurative opposite, standing in contrast to civilization as something hostile, natural and primitive. In this respect, like the Jungian shadow which contains our most base impulses and desires and is often unavailable to our conscious awareness, the Upside Down harbors those darker elements of human life that have been left behind, or are at least kept at bay, by the more civilized world of Hawkins as exemplified by the monsters that inhabit it.

The shadow is also something which, though its structure may be shared across people, its contents can differ.

> It is quite within the bounds of possibility for a man to recognize the relative evil of his nature, but it is a rare and shattering experience for him to gaze into the face of absolute evil. (p. 10)

This "absolute evil" is the evil that is common to all humanity. It is arguably what makes each one of us, given the right circumstances, capable of the most inhuman acts of barbarism and inhumanity.

Throughout the show, El is the flawed hero, in possession of supernatural abilities, who is capable of facing and conquering this absolute evil as embodied in the Demogorgon as seen at the end of both Seasons One and Two.

It takes a person with incredible mental and moral fortitude to confront the archetypal shadow, not just the personal shadow. As Jung points out, such people are incredibly rare. El is the only one capable of facing it and yet it still seems as if she is its equal. The ending of Season One is the act of seemingly mutual self-destruction which El is prey to when confronting the beast as they both seemingly disappear back into the Upside Down together. The fact that she is herself forced into the Upside Down suggests a strong connection between herself and the evil she defeats since they are ultimately banished to the same place.

## Self-Knowledge

The second episode of Season Two ("The Mall Rats") begins with a resurrection of sorts. The season starts by depicting the events at the end of Season One, just after the confrontation between El and the Demogorgon at the school in which El uses her powers to pin the monster to the blackboard and disintegrates the beast. At the start of Season Two, El pours out of the fleshy cavity which she has enlarged in the wall in order to make her way out from the Upside Down and back into the world. This is a symbolic rebirth and is in keeping with the Jungian theme of the individual emerging victorious over the darkest aspect of their nature.

Jung was keen to point out that there is precedent for concepts such as the shadow to be found in many of the world's mythologies (*Aion*, p. 34). Taking his cue from Jung, Ernest Becker points out that such depictions are commonplace in stories involving a hero's, in this case El's, journey into the unknown or into the underworld:

> Anthropological and historical research also began, in the nineteenth century, to put together a picture of the heroic since primitive and ancient times. The hero was the man who could go into the spirit world, the world of the dead, and return alive. He had his descendants in the mystery cults of the Eastern Mediterranean, which were cults of death and resurrection. The divine hero of each of these cults was one who had come back from the dead. (*The Denial of Death*, p. 12)

The spirit world or world of the dead may serve as proxies for the shadow. One of the purposes of going into the Upside Down, or confronting one's shadow side, is to harvest what may be found there. This is the point where self-knowledge takes on a particularly moral dimension.

In "The Upside Down," Officer Hopper goes into the Upside Down with Joyce and finds his daughter's toy lion down there. Through a series of flashbacks it is revealed that he feels responsible for being incapable of saving his dying daughter. In this scene in the Upside Down, he's thereby confronted with something from his past which he has been unable to put to rest and has been hiding from at the bottom of a glass.

To redeem himself from what he perceives as his failure to save his daughter, he is required to enter into the Upside Down. This is poignantly illustrated in the scene where he revives Will, which is contrastingly juxtaposed to the flashbacks of the failed attempts of the doctors to revive his daughter, for which he feels personal responsibility. Hopper has personal baggage and trauma which has not been put to rest and in this sense the Upside Down, like the shadow, contains those aspects of himself which he has been trying to escape from and has concealed away from himself. The redemptive quality of reconciling oneself with their shadow is thereby hinted at.

## The Relationship Between the Shadow and the Ego

There are occasional irruptions from the unconscious into consciousness (*Aion*, p. 8). This is first depicted in "Madmax," where Will, having disappeared into the Upside Down, is clearly attempting to communicate with his mother. Will first attempts to communicate via the telephone, then by flickering the fairy lights, and finally by playing a song of great significance in his brother's room in order to make it clear to his mother that it is her son trying to get in touch with her.

The song is significant as it is one of the first songs Will's brother played to him and put onto the mixtape he made for him. The message he is attempting to communicate is initially unclear, although this is a clear example of something attempting to make its way from the unknown and the unarticulated up into conscious awareness. The message he is trying to convey is a warning that the Demogorgon is about to come through into the world of Hawkins and that his mother should try to escape.

The unconscious sends all sorts of vapors, odd beings, terrors and deluding images up into the mind-whether in dream, broad daylight, or insanity; for the human kingdom, beneath the floor of the comparatively neat little dwelling that we call our consciousness, goes down into unsuspected Aladdin caves (*Hero with a Thousand Faces*, p. 8).

Technology serves as the medium by which the unknown is communicated, through lights, phones, CD players or the apparitions caught on video camera.

It is possible that a person identifies with, or becomes the same as, the shadow side of the unconscious. This is what happens to Will when he becomes possessed by the Demogorgon in "The Pollywog." Someone is susceptible to the ego becoming identified with the shadow when, "the ego lacks any critical approach to the unconscious. In that case it is easily overpowered and becomes identical with the contents that have been assimilated" (*Aion*, p. 23). This needn't happen all at once and it isn't until "The Spy," when Will loses his memory, that the transformation is complete.

Bob, Joyce's boyfriend in Season Two, comments that people like himself and Will don't fight back so people always get one over on them. Having this kind of passive personality, Will is fit to be overpowered by others and his possession by the Shadow Monster seems to indicate a certain lack of enough fortitude in his character. He is both timid and weak. This may sound like an unnecessarily harsh criticism but who can really stand their ground in the face of absolute evil, save someone with superhuman powers?

A person becomes her own shadow when she suppresses or refuses to acknowledge the contents of her unconscious shadow and is therefore unable to integrate these contents into her consciousness. Since the shadow remains unintegrated with the conscious ego, it is unable to fall under her conscious control. A failure to integrate unconscious contents serves to increase the scope and power of the unconscious's influence over the ego (*Aion*, p. 24). This is why Will and El make such interesting contrasts. Will, who is too weak to overcome the Shadow Monster, becomes an instrument of its evil. El on the other hand is able to use her otherworldly powers in order to defeat evil, as depicted at the end of each season when she defeats the Demogorgon and the Shadow Monster.

## The Moral Dimension Revisited

More can be said about the relationship between morality and the shadow:

> Certain virtues like attention, conscientiousness, patience etc., are of great value on the moral side, just as accurate observation of the symptomatology of the unconscious and objective self-criticism are valuable on the intellectual side. (*Aion*, pp. 24–25)

From a moral point of view, it is necessary to be a well-functioning human being. We should pay attention to those aspects of our unconscious that may overpower our ego and take control of our whole personality as represented in the case of Will. It is not that he's immoral to begin with but, being presented as weak and timid, he is unfit to stand up to the Shadow Monster.

This can be prevented by cultivating the moral and intellectual virtues. Amongst the virtues we would also list character traits such as courage and honesty. El exemplifies these two traits most of all. In "Will the Wise," El is disgusted by what she perceives as Hopper's dishonesty towards her, exclaiming, "Friends don't lie!" when he won't tell her how long it is before you can see Will again. Her bravery is shown in her ability to face down the Demogorgon and Shadow Monster.

El's relationship with her shadow is much more complicated than Will's. Her life and the monster's are, at the end of Season One, seemingly linked in death. El clearly has traits that are the same as a monster's. She hardly hesitates to kill the agents and accomplices of Hawkins National Laboratory. Although we may think that she's justified in killing her captors and tormentors, it is because of her monstrous nature that she is capable of doing so. She has powers that we do not recognize as being part of this world and it is this that makes her so dangerous. El treads a fine line between being capable of doing untold good or unspeakable evil. El therefore represents an uncomfortable marriage between her conscious ego and unconscious shadow, but one that is necessary for her to be the hero that she is.

## The Relationship between the Shadow and the Self and Identity

There's more to the self than just the conscious ego; the shadow is also necessary. Both parts are therefore incomplete by themselves. It's no wonder that the depiction of the monster in *Stranger Things* is something somewhat formless, yet nonetheless humanoid. It is primitive and reduced to the most basic of infantile functions as it is essentially little more than a body with a mouth, capable only of devouring.

As Joyce says in "The Body," commenting on the portrayal of the monster, "it was almost human but it wasn't. It had long arms and it didn't have a face." This fit perfectly with Jung's characterization of the shadow:

> On this lower level [of the personality] with its uncontrolled or scarcely controlled emotions one behaves more or less like a prim-

itive, who is not only the passive victim of his affects but also singularly incapable of moral judgment. (*Aion*, p. 9)

Given what we have said about self-knowledge, it's no mere coincidence that Season Two deals with El growing up after her symbolic rebirth. After coming out of the Upside Down at the end of Season One, El is like a timid animal more than a human being. The chief leaves food out for her, which she timidly approaches, confident that no one will be there to see her. From thereon she learns to speak properly, to eat, and to rebel, as teenagers are wont to do. She goes on to uncover her personal history once she has freed herself from her captors at Hawkins lab.

She has defeated the Shadow Monster in the Upside Down and now begins to uncover her identity to learn who she is. She has overcome her shadow for now, although she will face it again in the Season Two. The shadow is therefore an integral part of El's larger self which she has had to reconcile herself with in order truly come to know and develop her character.

## Every Ending Is a Beginning

The integration of the shadow is not a process that ever has a definitive endpoint. It is always possible that one could be overcome by the forces of darkness that lurk within. It is quite conceivable that El could have gone down a different route and used her powers for evil instead of good and just because she has reconciled the different sides to her personality for now, it doesn't mean that her shadow and conscious ego won't become separated again in the future.

As for Will, it is possible that now he has been rescued from the possession of the Shadow Monster, he will return with new moral and intellectual fortitude and virtue which will enable him to resist the forces of the Upside Down in the future.

We can expect that the shadow will throw up new challenges and monstrosities which will demand resolution and defeat. Season Two ends on a natural kind of resting place, a pause from the chaos and nightmares that have led El, or Jane, to better know herself and develop in accordance with this newfound self-knowledge. As Nietzsche puts it, she is here at the point of "becoming who she is" (*The Gay Science*, Aphorism 270).

# 11
# Not from Around Here

ANDREA ZANIN

Something is coming. Something hungry for blood. A shadow grows on the wall behind you, swallowing you in darkness. It is almost here.

—MIKE WHEELER, "The Vanishing of Will Byers"

It lives in the recesses of your mind, the deepest crevices of your subconscious—where it lurks, prowls . . . *waiting* for even a hint of weakness to acknowledge it into being. *It* is a shadow that scavenges on dark thoughts, turning order into chaos; sense into nonsense; a small-town girl into a psychokinetic, telepathic force of nature; or a Venus Flytrap into a humanoid xenomorph-thing that feasts on the blood of its prey. *It* is Fear. And Fear is rife. *Rife* but unpalatable. We know it's there—we sense it with our intuition but choke it down with our pragmatism. Yet it remains undaunted—it has other ways to get at us. Monsters, the children of Fear, are never gone; they manifest in discourse—art, literature, film, popular culture, episodes of *Stranger Things*—as minions of Horror, sent to remind us that when we stray from life's proverbial path or mess with the system, there will be a reckoning.

Like the mythology and the folk stories of old, Horror is a cautionary tale, an explanation; a warning—divert from the path and trouble will follow. When Icarus ignored his dad and flew too high, he died; when Little Red took a short cut through the wood, she met a furry fiend who ate her Gran;

when The Company ordered Ash to secret an Alien back to earth, the world nearly ended (God bless Ellen Ripley); and when Hawkins National Laboratory abducted children and experimented on them, the Demogorgon came to life and had townsfolk for dinner.

Buck the system or break the law and chaos will happen. And who likes chaos—as in *Lord of the Flies* (aka death and pig heads on sticks) kinda chaos, as opposed to an over-sub-scribed Funfair or an almost rowdy party? Uh . . . *no one*, right? Horror exposes the corruption of our souls and the effect this has on our lives and our world. As a genre it forces our mind into places it doesn't dare to go; it offers a safe space to contemplate the reckoning and by allowing us to feel relief with the hallucinatory context of imagination, we are reminded of the necessity of our own morality. In a way, Horror keeps us (humanity) in check by offering a *what if*, an alternate reality—usually a rubbish one. No thanks.

## A Plane Out of Phase

Coming face to face with the state of our own depravity is not only cringeworthy and deeply horrific but also ominous in epic proportion. When *Snow White*'s Evil Queen is faced with her insane vanity, she is frozen with rage . . . *and then* commanded by the prince to wear a pair of red hot iron slippers and dance in them until she drops dead. Nice. And when Oscar Wilde's Dorian Gray looks upon the portrait of his blackened soul, he effectively murders himself. "Take heed," the reflection says.

In *Stranger Things*, the Upside Down works like the Evil Queen's mirror and Dorian Gray's painting; offering another version of reality, a reflection of a world gone wrong. Likened to The Vale of Shadows (or Shadowfell, if we're going to be persnickety about Dungeons & Dragons mythological accu-racy), it's described in *Stranger Things* in Season One ("The Flea and the Acrobat") as "a dimension that is a dark reflec-tion, or echo, of our world. It is a place of decay and death, a plane out of phase, a place with monsters. It is right next to you and you don't even see it."

It's an allegory that offers insight into a broken world and a defective psyche through the metaphoric rendition of a fractured society, one where fathers show little interest in their children, parents fight and divorce, bullies take your stuff and break it (and also smash your head in); it's a place where racism abounds—a "hell hole," according to Will's dad (Oh, irony!) . . . and we're just talking Hawkins here; there's a whole world where this came from.

The Upside Down is a cold, dark, deathly place—is this what our world feels like? Could it be an example of a psychological abyss—the emotional and mental wretchedness resulting from a broken society? *Stranger Things* uses monsters to expose social disharmony in Hawkins and it is through the consideration of the concept of *monster* as an "analogy for understanding whatever the hell this is" (aptly enunciated by Dustin in "The Mind Flayer") that we gain greater insight into the fractious nature of the world at large—and exactly what we're supposed to do about it.

## May I Have Your Attention, Please?

*So,* . . . monsters—*Stranger Things* has some good 'uns; the dreaded Demogorgon, its bestial spawns—the demodogs, the Shadow Monster *aka* Mind Flayer . . . and then we have Eleven ('El' for short); and if we dump her into monster category, then Eight has to go there, too. And, well, if El and Eight are monsters, who's to say that Joyce, Hopper, Mike, Max (definitely her brother) and well, *people*—the regular kind—aren't equally monstrous? Uh . . . *say what?* El and the Demogorgon you, me . . . *everyone*)—one and the same? Well, here's a little FYI: the term 'monster' derives from the Latin word *monstrare* meaning to show forth or demonstrate . . . (let's finish the phrase with) . . . *monstrous behavior.* Translation: it's not only about looking gross. Fine. Except, I don't know about y'all but I sure as hell haven't feasted on anyone lately, or ever. (Insert scream-face emoji—*with your mind* because this is not a text or a Facebook post). Try to swallow your panic, it's okay, promise; there's method in the madness—his name is Foucault. Paul-Michel Foucault (1926–1984), to be exact: a French philosopher whose musings on the notion of *monster* will help us figure all this crazy-talk out.

Foucault was interested in the *abnormal* and in a series of lectures at the Collège de France (1974–1975). The philosopher delineates the subject of abnormality in the context of history, society, and law. In order to engage in a conversation on the abnormal, Foucault believed that the idea of monster must be investigated—because abnormality is typically associated with monstrousness of both essence and behavior. And so Foucault defined the notion of monster as an amalgamation of two parts: *morphological irregularity* and *transgression of law*. Essentially, for an entity to qualify as a monster, it must stand in violation of the laws of nature as well as the laws of society; thus contravening normality in both *essence* and *behavior.*

Scholars often refer to the *juridicio-natural* complex of Foucault's monster, or his bio-political monster—a being that is located and understood within the context of the law *(juridicio)* and nature *(natural)* and is rendered monstrous by defying the rules of both, making said being a combination of the impossible (physically) and the forbidden (legally) (*Abnormal*, p. 56). In his hypothesis on the emergence of abnormality, Foucault alludes to the fact that each culture and all historic periods breed monsters; that each age has its own "privileged monster" and that monsters are, in fact, cultural constructions—completely fictitious (the ugly kind), or a perversion of living flesh, an organic being (the human kind).

Mythological monsters tend to be entirely fictitious, much like the hellhound*ish* Demodogs in *Stranger Things*, whilst the Middle Ages is more partial to a man-beast sort of monster (rendered through the mixing of species), like the Demogorgon. The Renaissance focused on physical abnormalities typically resulting from gene irregularities—hermaphrodites or Siamese twins; and then in the contemporary era monstrosity changes from something physical to something mental or psychological—serial killers, psychopaths, individuals exhibiting pathological behaviour or perhaps even children with supernatural powers. *Stranger Things* almost plots the cultural evolution of the notion of monster as articulated by Foucault, starting with the mythological monster as inspiration for its own narrative.

## It Was Almost Human

Mythology is a collection of stories that were used to explain how a society's customs, taboos, and institutions (the social order, in other words) were established and sanctified. Mythology is ancient, as in before Christ ancient, and yet the Duffer brothers have drawn on the classic mythological monster to play out their modern-day horror epic. The Demogorgon and its canine cronies invoke Foucault's mention of mythical monsters that defy the real-world laws of nature and society, and in real life make no physical sense at all. They might seem natural in the alternate reality of the Upside Down, but not in Hawkins, Indiana 1980s—where laws mean jack to a slimy, skinny humanoid-creature with a rotting flower-face and killer teeth. The Demogorgon and Demodogs (and the Shadow Monster) subvert the laws of biology that govern the natural world and the creatures certainly do no obey the moral laws that form its overarching legal system—last time I checked, eating and possessing people . . . *not cool*, or legal.

And yet while the Demo-monsters are obviously fictitious (gross and otherworldly) and quite obviously bestial, they are also humanoid in some aspects—even the dogs. Joyce describes the Demogorgon in Season One ("The Body") as, "That thing . . . it was almost human but it wasn't; it had these long arms but it didn't have a face;" a point further emphasized by Nancy when she calls it "a guy with no face." As for the Demodogs, other than the creature's bizarre love of nougat, it displays a strange sort of humanism, like when it attacks and kills Bob in "The Mind Flayer"—pinning him down and lifting its claw-paw like a crazed but intentional killer in stab-mode, before hacking away at the poor soon-to-be-dead dude. And as bestial as this creature might be, it demonstrates a level of intelligence that responds to Dustin's care. When the gang runs into Dart (short for D'Artagnan) in the tunnels, he seems to demonstrate some sort of recognition and is easily manipulated with the whiff of a Three Musketeers candy bar *(of course)*. Bribed by chocolate? If that's not almost human then I don't know what is? Okay—slightly farfetched? But the utopian in all of us would like to think that dear Dart would've let Dustin pass without the lure of the combination of chocolate and nougat.

The Shadow Monster, also boss of the Underworld (and *hella* scary), further emphasizes the link between man and monster, as mentioned in Foucault's theory as being typical of the thinking that went on in the Middle Ages. Dustin likens the Shadow Monster to the Mind Flayers from Dungeons & Dragons, which were denizens of the "Underdark" (a vast network of underground caverns and tunnels underneath the surface of Abeir-Toril—*much like the labyrinth happening under Hawkins*) and were also known as "mind rulers."

These sadistic beings are described as alien humanoid-looking aberrations sought to expand their dominion over all other creatures, controlling their minds to use them as hopeless slaves and devouring their brains for sustenance (Forgotten Realms Wiki 2018). In *Stranger Things*, the Shadow Monster possesses Will, who tells Mike ("Dig Dug"), "It's like I know what the Shadow Monster is feeling; see what he's seeing . . . Some of him is there in the Upside Down but some of him is here too; in this house and in me. It's like he's reaching into Hawkins more and more, and the more he spreads, the more connected to him I feel." This Mind Flayer guy is taking over Will and soon, the boy will be the beast—leaving a monster that looks much like you and much like me.

## Girl Power

Perhaps less obvious bio-political monsters because they're not all dastardly and disgusting, El and Eight are guilty nonetheless of breaching laws both natural and political. Naturally, El and Eight are not normal; intrinsic to their makeup is the ability to control the minds of people and things (in varying and differing degrees), much like the Mind Flayer. Their brain composition and functionality goes against the norm and slots them into the realm of the abnormal. They are a biological breach of nature, even though they might not look it. And as far as breaking the law, well . . . Eight's a robber, murderer, and all-round badass. And El? Her unofficial rap sheet includes grievous bodily harm, reckless endangerment, destruction of property *etcetera*—El's been a naughty girl. Some of El's infractions might have occurred in mitigating circumstances—to save lives and preserve freedoms—but for Foucault, it is simply the co-presence of these two forms of breach (biological and political) that account for the birth of monsters. But if Foucault can't quite convince you that these girls are a tad monster, what about Lucas, who, in an argument with Mike after El has tossed him through the air with her mind powers (as she does), says (more like yells), "We're looking for some stupid monster! But did you ever stop to think that maybe *she's* the monster?" ("The Flea and the Acrobat").

If we can then agree that the aforementioned creatures and characters of *Stranger Things* conform to Foucault's notion of *monster*, what's more interesting is *why* they have been used as an integral part of the show. The obvious answer—to scare the shit out of us. Great—goal achieved! But these monsters are not entirely gratuitous; *Stranger Things* is more sophisticated than that.

## It Takes One to Know One

*Stranger Things* begs us to delve deeper by pointing to its own allegory. Dungeons & Dragons (*The* role-play game of the 1980s) is a clear reference point within the show—Mike and the gang play D&D and they use D&D as a go to when explaining the loony stuff that happens in Hawkins, like: the Demogorgon, who is the Prince of Demons and has been an iconic creature in D&D mythology since 1975; the Shadow Monster is likened to the Mind Flayer in the game, and even the term 'psionic'—which, in D&D mythology, is a source of power that originates from within a being's mind, allowing it to augment its physical abilities and affect the minds of other creatures (*hello*—El and Eight!).

By seeing such clear allegorical references within the show, viewers cannot help but perceive *Stranger Things* within the context of the allegorical; as an allusion to real life. So, when we ask the question *why* these specific creatures, which seem to amalgamate human and monster into one; the answer is that they serve as a mechanism of the cautionary tale that is horror. They are literal representations of humans as monsters—alluding to the fact that monstrousness is not only characterized by obvious physical repulsiveness but can also be housed in the physical innocuousness of human beings. Let's not deceive ourselves or one another—we are bad, as bad as it gets.

Take, for example Billy Hargrove—Max's stepbrother. What an ass! He treats his sister badly—bullying her and her friends—threatening them, hating on Lucas because he's black, and beating Steve to an almost bloody pulp. Because he can. And also, because *monkey see, monkey do*—Billy learns his abusive ways from his father (another bad guy)—as seen in Season Two's "The Mind Flayer" when his dad hits him in response to his bad attitude.

Will and Jonathan's dad, Lonnie, also sucks; he forced Jonathan to kill a rabbit (scarring the poor kid for life); called Will "queer" and a "fag;" and after he and Joyce divorced, made little effort to stay in contact with his sons. He's also a drunkard, bully, and major sleaze, or *monster* (the human kind) if you're channelling Foucault in the modern era.

And what about El's Papa? Kidnapper and abuser of children. El was stolen from her mother, raised in isolation, manipulated and threatened into compliance, and taught to kill (that episode with the cat. . . . *so wrong*—"Holly, Jolly"). Human rights attorneys and family advocates would have a field day with this case study.

Even Mike and the gang are assholes to each other (breaking the "friends do not lie" code—when Dustin hides his pet Demogorgon from the group—as one example), and Steve and Jonathan also have their moments (camera breaking, bullying, and girlfriend stealing); does this make them monsters within the confines of Foucault's theory? Perhaps not. In the context of *Stranger Things*, these characters mostly break a moral code rather than a political one. There's nothing to suggest that their physical or psychological character is unnatural or abnormal in any way—and yet the show begs us to impose upon them the notion of monster.

In his lectures on the abnormal, Foucault described the monster as a being in which the mixture of two kingdoms can be seen. He was referring, in particular, to the bestial monster (which is a mishmash of human and animal), but this concept can be applied symbolically and metaphorically when perceived in light of the mythology that informs the narrative of *Stranger Things*. We have a bunch of monsters. Some are human with strange abnormalities (El and Eight); some are bestial with humanoid characteristics (the Demogorgon and Demodogs); and some are just regular who behave like asses (monstrously), like Papa and Will's dad—all of which represent the idea that humans (the regular kind) are not much different from the 'monster' Foucault fears. These monsters (all of them) traverse kingdoms—Hawkins and the Upside Down—and bear characteristics of both places. By insinuating the philosophical sameness of El and the Demogorgon, human and monster are brought closer together; *Stranger Things* forces us to question ourselves, our behaviors, our ethics and the way in which we exist in the world.

## The Weirdo on Maple Street

The Demogorgon (and the Upside Down) is brought into the earthly realm by El, who is experimented on by the scientists at Hawkins National Laboratory as part of project MK-Ultra (also called the CIA Mind Control Program). El is born telekinetic but is taken away from her mother at birth and raised in the laboratory as a test subject in order to develop her psychokinetic skills. Project MK-Ultra was a real thing, existing outside of the context of *Stranger Things*. It lasted from 1953 until about 1973 and was a top-secret CIA project in which the agency conducted hundreds of clandestine experiments—sometimes on unwitting US citizens—to assess the potential use of LSD and other drugs for mind control, information gathering, and psychological torture ("MK-Ultra"); an obvious infraction of human rights and legal principles.

According to Foucauldian discourse, monsters appear whenever and wherever knowledge/power assemblages emerge—in this instance we have the abuse of power (Hawkins lab) and we have the emergence of the Demogorgon (Demodogs and Shadow Monster), brought into existence by El, who, when placed in a sensory deprivation tank, is able to engage in astral projection and access other dimensions (for the purposes of international espionage, of course). On the evening of November 6th 1983, El encounters a creature living in the Upside Down and makes contact with it and in so doing opens a gate between Hawkins lab and the Upside Down, giving the Demogorgon the ability to traverse worlds. *Oops.*

Here's the caution: break the law, and chaos ensues. The monsters that emerge from the Upside Down wreak havoc on the town of Hawkins and its residents, on a visceral level—maiming, killing, and forcing death through decay. In an essay entitled *La monstruosité et le monstrueux*, Georges Canguilhelm (a French philosopher who is known to have been an inspiration to Foucault) affirms that the monster puts at issue the power of life to teach us order—by disrupting the path and messing with the system—and that this creates a radical fear because monstrosity could have been produced in us. When we deviate from the code, or the law, we encounter our own innate fallibility and corruptibility— our abnormality. This is the exact thing that *Stranger Things*—as a cog in the great wheel of Horror—implies; that we all have a little bit (or a lot) of monster in us. Just think about El; test subject, opener of the gate, nose bleeder, lifter of toy spaceships, flipper of cars, killer of lab technicians, vanquisher of the Demogorgon . . . oh, and savior. That's right—it's complicated. *People are complicated.*

Remember the part in the show when El's watching *Frankenstein* (1931)? She's sitting on a sofa, cuddling a teddy to her chest. In the clip, a little girl says: "Who are you? I'm Maria . . . Will you play with me?" And Frankenstein's monster looks blankly at Maria, and then the girl and monster wander off hand in hand. It's a beautiful and poignant moment as El's winsome expression acknowledges a crisis in identity; she's caught between both characters on screen— monster and girl—and has to navigate the reality of perhaps being a bit of both. She's probably also trying to figure out what the heck it means to *play*—poor little lab-baby. And speaking of living dead things, Will Byerses' nickname at school (thanks to the shenanigans told of in *Stranger Things* Season One) is "Zombie Boy"—another human-monster allusion; it's a point belabored by many of the peripheral references that proliferate in the show, including a shout out to Michael Myers (arch nemesis and psychopath) when Max dresses up as the super psycho on Halloween night ("Trick or Treat"). Also, "Will Byers" / "Mike Myers" —just saying . . .

## Get Over It!

It is through the character of the complicated monster figure, that Foucault is able to comment on human nature. The philosopher talks about the "the monster from below and the monster from above" and says that in their very twinship, these two figures will haunt the problematic of abnormal individuality (p. 1). The truth is that we've all got a little bit of the Upside Down in us, whether we go around breaking the law or not. But if we do break the law, and move from the realm of abnormal into the realm of criminal—showing preference to our own interest rather than the law (p. 92)—what should we do about it?

Some sort of penal incursion or prison something-or-other. That's right—send the Demogorgon to jail, that'll work . . . *don't feel bad imagining another inappropriate emoji face here*—the one with laughter and tears superimposed onto the wide-eyed *WTF* face would be most apt. The thing is, the Demogorgon has no right to be automatically subscribed to society's mores and values. The creature is from another dimension and as a being of monstrous nature and the enemy of the whole of society, shouldn't society get rid of it without calling upon the might of the law (as per Foucault)? So, what do we do with the dastardly creature then? According to *Stranger Things*—pick up a bigass baseball bat with nails sticking out of it (like that crazy Pin Head guy from *Hellraiser*) and beat that Demogorgon and its dogish fiends to smithereens. Or set El on the monsters—that works a treat.

Much like the Demogorgon, mightn't the monstrous criminal (who is by his very nature bad) be excluded from the social pact—a natural consequence of existing in the world—by virtue of his/her/its/their biological abnormality? Like Michael Myers; a born psychopath, suffering brain impairment attributed to fetal alcohol syndrome and autism too, which, along with environmental stressors, activated voyeuristic and murderous tendencies (RealClearScience 2019) turning him into a killer . . . *as an example*? What does society do with such a fiend? The real-life equivalent of a spiked bat might be the death penalty or the more humane option of a mental institution—a home for the abnormal? Both are mechanisms of a legal system and thus not entirely appropriate for those existing in a metaphoric plane out of phase.

The potential for the injustice of such punishment is elicited through the contemplative fate of El, who was born in defiance of nature but made into a criminal by the power assemblages that incited her lawbreaking habit. Should El be put to death or institutionalized? Perhaps we digress with all this *what should we do with the bad guys stuff*. It's pretty obvious that the Demogorgon is not going to stand up in a court of law and be tried by a judge or jury (of its peers) . . . so, what then? Vigilantism?

Would Foucault approve of the guerrilla warfare approach adopted by *Stranger Things*? Without delving too deep into a leviathan topic, put it this way: a diverse group of scholars have accused Foucault of excessively downplaying the role of law in modern society by depicting legal discourse as a façade, with little power and ability to protect people from external interferences. And remember; the CIA (charged with protecting national security) and its dodgy MK-Ultra project is in part responsible for the very *external interference* in question. Anyone trust these guys to serve and protect? Right. So, the answer is *yes*—in the world of *Stranger Things*, if the law is not likely to prove powerful or effective in keeping chaos at bay, maybe Foucault would approve. Also, just a reminder THE DEMOGORGON'S NOT FROM AROUND HERE. Our law won't work regardless of what Foucault thinks. *And if all else fails* karma usually has its way; with many of the other bad guys in the show (Papa, the Demogorgon and co.) getting their just deserts.

It would be interesting to know how the Duffer brothers would deal with Eight, whose moral conscience seems to have been warped by her rage against the machine that created her (Hawkins Lab and its harbingers of injustice), thus invalidating the mitigation of her laboratory upbringing. An interesting conundrum . . . yet more important than what we do with the monster is the nature of its behavior in, as far as *Stranger Things* is concerned, at least.

## It's Called Being Human

The show recognizes the monster in humans but, in an ironic twist of philosophy, seems to punish it as well as embrace it. El, who is an assimilation of human and monster, does not receive the same just deserts as most of the other monsters in the show; instead El is the epic hero. What's also interesting to note here is that in Hebrew, names with "El" in them denote "God" or deity. It's a provocative comment that seems to vindicate the complexity of the human condition, as a messy, but okay, mix of monstrous and magnificent . . . *again*, it's complicated.

Will, who is made out to be a sort of vessel, or conduit—open to the darkness and the influences of evil—could easily be construed as weak but he is described by his friends as having "truesight" in an episode tellingly titled "Will the Wise." *Truesight*, as per D&D lore, is the ability to see in magical darkness, to see invisible creatures and objects, to automatically detect visual illusions, and perceive the original form of a shape changer or a creature that is transformed by magic. Furthermore, one with truesight can see into the Ethereal Plane. Rather than a weakness, this is considered some kind of superpower.

While Will feels like a "freak," Jonathan argues that "being a freak is the best" because "nobody normal ever accomplished anything meaningful in this world" ("The Weirdo on Maple Street"). Now, this might sound a touch *jejune*—meager, naive, crazy(!?)—all things considered, but the philosophical observation is that abnormality is a virtue, knowing the monster and what it's capable of builds strength, and is a weapon against fear. Bring it out of the darkness and into the light. That weirdo on Maple Street—it's you, me, all of us (plus a Demogorgon or two); it's time to stop being mouth-breathing wastoids and own it.

# 12
# Who Is Will Byers?

KYLE A. HAMMONDS AND CYNTHIA K. GORDON

Young Will Byers seems like the universe's punching bag in the dark world of *Stranger Things*. No amount of fun Eighties nostalgia or depictions of cute middle-school relationships can distract us from the fact that Will is pretty much always having a bad time.

Will spends most of Season One trapped in the Upside Down, enduring a frightening alternate universe until he is saved in an exciting last-chance rescue staged by his stalwart posse of family and friends. Will's luck appeared to be improving at the beginning of Season Two until he discovered through nightmares, visions, and unusual bodily functions that he may have brought a little piece of the Upside Down home with him during his escape.

As viewers progress through Season Two they find that Will was being gradually possessed by a mysterious and malevolent entity from the Upside Down—an entity not-so-affectionately named the "Mind Flayer" by Will's friends, after an evil, psionic Dungeons & Dragons character.

As viewers, we may learn quite a bit by considering the matter of Will's possession. Particularly, the issue of possession may bring up some questions about Will's identity. Is Will *really* Will if his body is being controlled by another entity? The answer to that question depends on who's being asked. Will, his friends, and his broader community may all have different ways of understanding his identity.

# Meet Zombie Boy

Much of what we know about Will comes from discussions amongst characters, especially Will's friends Mike, Dustin, and Lucas during Season One. They often express how much they care about and miss Will while he is away in the Upside Down. Season Two sees the group struggle with how to interact with Will after he returns from the Upside Down, though. While the kids generally seem to be glad for Will's return, they also treat him with caution and seem unsure of whether Will has fully recovered from his terrifying experience. Perhaps the clearest commentary on how other kids felt after Will returned from the Upside Down comes from a new nickname and a new addition to the close-knit group in the second season.

Season Two kicks off with the addition of a new character, Maxine "Madmax" Mayfield. Immediately embraced by Lucas and Dustin, they push Mike to include her in their "Party." Max is intrigued by Will, the oft-taunted "Zombie Boy." News about Will's disappearance early in Season Two added to Max's curiosity, as did Mike's refusal to let Lucas and Dustin share details of what she began to suspect was a rather big deal. Eventually Max learns Will's story: He went missing, he had a funeral, and all of a sudden, he returned. Hence, *Zombie Boy*.

When Mr. Clarke shares the story of Phineas Gage in science class, Max begins to realize there may be more to Will's story than she was initially told. Phineas was a railway worker who survived having an iron rod go through his head. The teacher concludes the story by saying that Phineas, "seemed fine . . . and physically, yes, he was. But his injury resulted in a complete change to his personality. So much so that friends that knew him started referring to him as No-Longer-Gage" ("The Pollywog"). As Max listens to the story and stares at Will, she considers whether Will, like Phineas, could ever be the same after his traumatic past. Her perceptions of the Zombie Boy were cynical, calling Will's current identity into question based on comparisons to what she understands about his past.

Meanwhile, Will's friends cling to the belief that Will is still, you know, *Will*. The version of him that they've known. As the show unfolds, we learn that a major concern for virtually all of the people in Will's life is whether the "old" and "new" Will are the same and, by extension, if they can predict how the new Will fits into their expectations and perceptions of the old Will.

The character anxieties related to Will's identity may also resonate with viewers of the show. Surely we have all had the experience of noticing changes in ourselves or in others and second-guessing our own identity. The questions "Who am I?" or "Who are you?" are challenging to answer and may be to blame for some serious dread. The idea that we're individuals with the freedom to choose how we act sometimes collides with the roles we're expected to play, causing us to question our own value in the world. Exploring Will's identity also gives us an opportunity to explore ourselves.

## Who Am I? Who Are You? Does It Really Matter?

We know some facts about Will now, but do facts about his life really tell us *who* he is? Perhaps a particular tool from sociological philosophy can help us learn a few things about Will's identity. *Symbolic interactionism* is a term that describes a paradigm, or philosophical point of view, for comprehending social identity, or in other words, an identity based on group membership. For example, one of Will's identities is established by his membership in the gaming culture. Because symbolic interactionists look at identity in terms of communally constructed meaning, we can safely assume that Will's understanding of his gamer identity comes from his experiences and interactions with other gamers as well as the attributions applied to him by non-gamers.

Symbolic interactionism tries to understand how people use symbols, such as words, to construct their perceptions of reality and then behave in response to those perceptions. The framework assumes that: 1. symbols allow us to express our perceptions and understanding of the world; 2. our perceptions of the world are informed by our interactions with others; and 3. our interactions alter our understanding of reality, which can influence our behavior. Symbolic interactionism was popularized by George Herbert Mead and continues to be used as a framework in social sciences such as sociology, social psychology, and communication studies.

## Symbolic Interactionism and Will's Identity

In regard to Will himself, symbolic interactionism helps us see Will's struggle with accepting change. The audience can clearly observe that he is not exactly the same as before his trip to the Upside Down (much like Mr. Clarke's analogy in "The Pollywog").

Will puts on a strong face, but lives in almost perpetual fear because of his nightmares about the Upside Down. Experience has changed him. His friends and family seem to treat him differently after he returns too. They walk on eggshells around him. They treat him as if he were broken. An example comes from Season Two ("Madmax") in which Will explodes to his brother, Jonathan, "Stop treating me . . . like everyone else does. Like there's something wrong with me . . . They all treat me like I'm gonna break." Another example, the protectiveness of Will's mom, Joyce, is communicated with particular clarity when she hesitates to let Will participate in trick-or-treating for Halloween in Season Two ("Trick or Treat, Freak").

Symbolic interactionism's assumption that other people ascribe their beliefs to our identities—helps to explain the coddling from Will's family. His family and friends, like many of us with our own friends and family, want to more-or-less know Will's identity. If we can ascribe certain qualities to someone, we feel confident that we know what to expect from them and how to interact with them. When people change and behave in ways that seem "out of character," our uncertainty increases and we might feel unsure or uncomfortable interacting with them. Joyce's protectiveness for Will only intensifies after Will begins scribbling images from his nightmares of the Upside Down in Season Two ("Will the Wise").

Will's relationships are at stake as he grapples with how to act around his family and friends in the wake of his return from the Upside Down. In the midst of Season Two, Will knows that he is changing. He has a nightmarish connection to the Upside Down and he has been terrorized by his experiences there. As much as he may want his life to go back to normal, Will also can't escape the fact that other people see him differently after his return. He's Zombie Boy, apparently a person to be either pitied or pushed away. Neither of those options seem to appeal to Will, though.

Will's struggle to be the same "Will" that his family and friends expect while also handling the changes in his own life are further complicated by the fact that a foreign consciousness followed Will back from the Upside Down in Season Two ("Madmax"). This Mind Flayer has a mind of its own even though it shares Will's body. Will's possession by the Mind Flayer brings up important questions for symbolic interactionists. If the consciousness of the Mind Flayer is working through Will's body, isn't that *still* Will? Does a transformation or change in behavior make someone *not themselves*?

Scholars, such as Mead, have argued that people cling to a handful of basic personality anchors for coherence and consistency. When people refer to the self, they are usually referring to these relatively stable anchors. If we try to remain stable in certain aspects of our identity, then we might feel more comfortable making decisions because we will believe that we have sure footing from which to move forward. These personality anchors also help others know what to expect from us when they're around us. Ultimately, we develop these personality anchors—even if they are subject to potential change over time. They reduce uncertainty. They give us confidence in taking future action.

Will generally continues playing the role of fragile little boy to Joyce. He presumably does this because he knows that his mom primarily relates to him by taking care of him. Conversely, Will lashes out at Jonathan when his brother also treats Will in a way that is similar to Joyce. When Jonathan tries to interact with Will based on beliefs about Will's enduring fragility, Will promptly tells Jonathan (as already quoted from "Madmax") to not treat him like he's going to break. Will attempts to negotiate a different sense of identity with Jonathan—one in which he's not simply reduced to a victim—and does so by means of interaction. In this case, talking with his brother was the key tool for interaction.

So, who is Will? Luckily, our role as omniscient viewers allows us to engage in a little armchair philosophy. The camera gives us enough information to understand that Will is basically content. He doesn't need or like to be the center of attention. He feels safe and fairly confident within his group of friends and is happy to go along with their ideas. A quiet boy, content to observe, and comfortable with his own thoughts.

Will's presentation of his self to others gives the audience a way to understand his identity by what he chooses to reveal to others (and what the show's creators choose to reveal to us). One way of making sense of identity is to follow Aristotle's rule, as summed up by Will Durant, "We are what we repeatedly do." However, Will's habits, his typical actions, are changed after he's possessed by the Mind Flayer. When the possession occurs, is he still Will or has he become the Mind Flayer? Or has Will become something entirely new?

Our identities seem to be a mish-mash of perceptions of ourselves, formed and honed by the interactions we have with others. Joyce's performance of protective mother is likely influenced by interactions with a traumatized Will who in turn creates an identity of needy child through their interactions. Each of them appears to shape the others' perception of self through interaction. In "Madmax," we see Joyce unable or unwilling to let Will out of her sight unless he has been handed off to someone else. In turn, these behaviors reinforce Will's belief that he is unable to take care of himself and needs constant protection. As Joyce hovers and Will accepts her protective shield, Joyce's perception of herself as protector is reinforced while Will's molding into the role of fragile child becomes solidified.

When we interact with others, we come to realize their expectations of us and either passively accept those expectations or endeavor to change them. Developing these expectations, or "anchors," is important to maintaining relationships, though, because they offer a base of experience from which to operate. It is hard to imagine that Joyce would know exactly how to communicate with Will after his return from the Upside Down if she couldn't fall back on how she best knew Will (as her little boy). Even so, as Will demonstrated by his resistance to Jonathan's over-protectiveness, the self is up for negotiation, both by ourselves and others. The persistence of a few relatively stable identity anchors—things we can expect about ourselves or others—help provide the foundations of our relationships.

Will's identity anchors are thoroughly challenged as the second season progresses. Instead of merely grappling with the tension between being recognizably the "old Will" to his family and friends *and* processing how he had changed since his experience in the Upside Down, Will further struggled with the presence of a vastly different consciousness fighting for control of his body.

In "The Mind Flayer" we see Will tied up in a shed with Joyce, Jonathan, Hopper, and Mike. These members of his friends and family, realizing the influence of the Mind Flayer, had imprisoned him with the hope that they could help him shake loose of the creature from the Upside Down. Each of the characters recounted personal stories to Will, trying to reach down past the evil possessing him to find the Will they believe is still inside. The version of Will which emerged from the influence of the Mind Flayer was frighteningly unrecognizable to his family and friends. Even though the Mind Flayer and Will combination character was, in a sense, simply the most recent version of Will, the people close to him wished to recover some of his old identity anchors (ideally the non-malicious stuff that got left behind after the Mind Flayer took over). This version of Will was nearly unrecognizable based on his family's previous experience and they did not know how to safely interact with him.

In this episode, the audience gets to experience Joyce's perception of Will directly as she tells him stories to encourage the version of Will that she recognized to fight the Mind Flayer's possession. She tells him of a little girl crying in a sandbox and young Will giving her his toy truck even though they didn't have money to replace the toy. She also tells the story of his first big box of crayons given to him on his eighth birthday, his preference for the crayons over other toys, and his drawing of a spaceship that she took to work and showed to everyone. Joyce's stories convey a particular perception of Will as a kind, perhaps fragile, creative child—a budding artist. She clearly saw such qualities as identity anchors which she associated with her interactions with Will. Joyce, and others, therefore interacted with Will in such a way as to try and draw forth the parts of him that were comfortable and familiar.

Symbolic interactionism relies on the connection between two key areas in order to develop understandings of identity.

The first area is a person's own experience of the self, which is usually expressed in habitual behaviors. The other area is how a person responds to the expected roles that they are called into by their friends and family. In other words, the self emerges from the interplay of constant interactions with others. We learn who we are by engaging other people, reflecting on our interactions, and making choices about how to present ourselves to others in the future. What this means for understanding Will is that we must consider his interactions with others in order to discover who he is in each context.

When Will interacts with Joyce, he usually plays the role of fragile child. With his friends, he is often the quiet one. To his classmates, he is Zombie Boy. Will is not simply any single one of those things, but people often look for relatively stable aspects of others' performances (such as Joyce's perception of Will's fragility) to understand how to respond to them.

The self is not necessarily a stable entity that we decide on, but, instead, a role that emerges in context and through communication. This being the case, the matter becomes much more complex for symbolic interactionists after the Mind Flayer exerts significant influence over Will's body. If the self is emergent, why not just accept each version of Will as he exists? For Will's friends and family, the answer is that they have invested their mind and heart into understanding Will in a certain way. If Will radically changes his values and actions based on the influence of the Mind Flayer, his family will be met with extreme uncertainty, and perhaps even repulsion, because they won't be able to recognize any of the identity anchors that they have previously associated with Will.

Once the Mind Flayer took over, the old version of Will ceased to exist—we are never a self from the past, but always presently existing. Even so, Will's family hoped to incorporate some of their expectations from past experience into the present after Will's possession. They desperately sought some semblance of coherence. His friends and family may have been willing to accept that Will is not simply *one thing*, such as a son, or brother, or friend; but they may understandably feel challenged to accept a version of Will which is not *any of those things* which had come to be associated with Will's identity.

## Identity Lessons

During the unfolding of Will's possession by the Mind Flayer in Season Two, Will's volition and agency over his own body decreases in response to his connection to the monster. At this point, Will was, in one sense, merely changing as he began interacting with others around him in new ways; however, the elements of fantasy in *Stranger Things* also complicate aspects of Will's change.

Whereas most people in real life have general unity of thought and can cling to a set of relatively stable identity anchors (such as things we perceive to be core values that we hold on to across most contexts), Will's consciousness was not as much replaced by a new self, the Mind Flayer, as it was preserved and suppressed. This is not really something we expect to see in real life situations, but it makes for excellent drama and brings up surprising aspects of identity for the audience to consider. During Will's possession—especially as culminating in "The Mind Flayer"—a consciousness maintaining one set of identity anchors that had been cultivated through interaction with Will's family (generally presented to the audience as the real Will) seemed to exist simultaneously with a malevolent consciousness featuring an entirely different set of identity anchors (the destructive Mind Flayer).

As Will mentioned to his doctor, the influence of the Mind Flayer began to seem almost omnipresent to him: "I felt it. Everywhere. *Everywhere*. I—I still feel it" ("Will the Wise"). The increase of the Mind Flayer's presence through Will generates conflict among major characters as to whether the body of the young boy could still be identified as Will—or whether the body had become a soulless vessel of the Mind Flayer. Ultimately, the conflict is a look into tensions that result from negotiating the self with others

One aspect of symbolic interactionism demonstrated in *Stranger Things* is that the self has stable anchors, but unstable characteristics. There are abstract aspects of the self that we might choose to cling to, but our actions are subject to change in our environment. Will held himself to general values such as honesty and the importance of community. He demonstrated these qualities in various ways. An example of Will's commitment to honesty comes from his introduction in the series in which he is playing Dungeons & Dragons with his friends. He rolls a pair of dice to determine whether he would succeed in overcoming a particular challenge of the game, but the dice fell on the ground where the dungeon master, Mike, (the narrator and organizer of the game) could not see the results of the roll. Lucas encouraged Will to be dishonest about the unfavorable results of his roll, but Will admitted the true results to Mike. Further, Will's consistent attention to spending time with his friends, including playing Dungeons & Dragons, convey his special interest in spending time with his community of comrades.

His ability to enact these values was eventually interrupted by the Mind Flayer, but this adverse influence also created an opportunity for a new version of Will to emerge. For instance, Will often plays the fragile child in response to his friends and family who perceive him as something that's "gonna break" ("Madmax") or as the weird Zombie Boy. After being possessed by the Mind Flayer, though, Will has to gather courage and choose to act, despite expectations of fragility, in order to work with his peers to defeat the monster.

Although the invading consciousness of the Mind Flayer had primary control over Will's body, his friends and family treated him as if there were stable identity anchors from his past which could be pulled forward into the present version of Will. The primary example of this treatment comes in "The Mind Flayer" episode, in which Will's family reminisces with him using stories his past which demonstrated qualities he had previously exhibited that they found to be admirable. Eventually, after Joyce's talk of Will's early childhood kindness toward other kids and similar talks from Jonathan and Hopper, Will began to present qualities of a self that he had constructed with his family in earlier interactions—the kind and honest child that others already knew and loved.

By drawing on such memories, the emergent Will became closer to his previous constructions of self and less like the Mind Flayer. In other words, Will's major values never changed through his ordeal with the Mind Flayer, but his method of playing the role of child or brother adjusted based on contextual needs. When Will's family urged the kinder consciousness in his body to resist the powerful malevolent force, they jointly communicated a version of Will which was still kind and honest, but that was less fragile and more able to make his own choices.

Will at the end of Season Two is extremely similar to Will at the start of the season, in that he still seems to hold the same basic values; but he is also different in that he renegotiated how he played a son to Joyce or a brother to Jonathan by drawing on their encouragement and then enacting his family's hopes that he could overcome the evil influence of the Mind Flayer. We have some control over how we present ourselves to others (such as Will deciding on what behaviors go into playing the part of a son or a brother), but we also make choices in response to other people (such as Will trying to meet other people's expectations of who he could or should be).

*Stranger Things* offers us a sort of eerie optimism regarding identity threats. Will experienced social trauma after his journey to the Upside Down in Season One. This experience maximized his reputation as fragile and shy while minimizing his initiative and self-control. However, these experiences were not demonstrated to be all-powerful. They influenced the way that Will presented himself to others, but the circumstances were not so constraining that he couldn't change.

Will eventually constructed a version of himself with his friends and family which was still familiar to them, but was less fragile and more capable than how he previously presented himself. He seemed to accomplish this by first *realizing* his agency. He had to recognize that he had the ability to act in his social environment and exert influence on others. Even though Will spends much of Season Two responding to the expectations exerted on him by others—by remaining the quiet, weird Zombie Boy or accepting all of his mother's protective doting—he found during his battle with the Mind Flayer that his choices mattered and he could perform outside of his generally assigned fragile-child role.

Will had help in realizing his agency. His friends and family rallied together with him and accepted the possibility that he could do more than idly accept the presentation of self invoked by the Mind Flayer. Beyond just realizing his potential ability to change, though, Will also had to *actualize* his agency. In other words, it was not enough for Will to understand that he could change, but he also had to actually enact the changes that he wanted to see in himself.

Again we see that the self emerges from the communicative exchange between several persons. So, Will's community could certainly influence his efficacy in making changes. If Will's family and friends had rejected his efforts to present himself without the influence of Mind Flayer, he might have relented in those efforts and reverted to the Mind Flayer version. Fortunately, Will's community was supportive of his desire to break out of the role of fragile child and acknowledged his ability to make changes.

By the end of Season Two, Will conveys significant courage and initiative in collaborating with others to defeat the Mind Flayer. In the final analysis, *Stranger Things* shows us that, while the influence of others is important, we may also find opportunities to grow out of undesirable social expectations. Learning about Will helps us, the audience, to also learn about the self. In Will, we see a person who was considerably influenced by the expectations of others. Just like Will, much of what we believe about ourselves undoubtedly comes from our experiences with other people—especially people who we view as being important to us. We tend to enjoy the comfort and routine that comes with ritualistically playing the roles ascribed to us. These roles are not necessarily set in stone, though.

Just like how Will realized that he could overcome perceptions of others (and even himself) that he must consistently play the fragile child before he actually took action to combat that perception, we can also realize and actualize changes in our own lives. We can do this by imagining new versions of ourselves, taking action toward change, and influencing our peers to collaborate with us as we enact those changes. As with Will, change is certainly easier with the support of peers who help us form our impressions of self, but we certainly have the power to affect how others see and interact with us as well.

Will's story in *Stranger Things* encouragingly suggests that identity can be recognizable and can feature some stability, but is certainly not unchangeable.

# V

---

## *How Do We Cope with the Strange?*

# 13
# Kids on Civil Disobedience

ENZO GUERRA AND ADAM BARKMAN

Many of the characters in *Stranger Things*, such as Mike, Dustin, Lucas, Madmax, and Chief Hopper, encounter laws, rules, and regulations throughout their endeavor to combat the forces of the Upside Down, but they don't always follow these laws, and perhaps rightly so. Although it may appear that these kids are just being mischievous rebels who don't care about rules, in many cases they actually have valid reasons to break the ones they do.

This is not to say that everything they did was the best choice, but rather that they acted in the right manner. This often caused them to face many risks—dangerous ones that could have led to many terrible consequences. Despite these risks, these characters nonetheless continually acted upon their moral intuitions to do the right thing.

## When Is It Right to Break the Rules?

The characters in *Stranger Things* often break the law, and break other rules of society, in ways that we feel to be right. They are practicing what we call civil disobedience.

Henry David Thoreau, a well-known nineteenth-century American essayist and philosopher, wrote about laws and our relationship towards them, especially in his book *Civil Disobedience*. Writing during the time of American slavery and the American-Mexican war (1846–1848), Thoreau argues that when laws are unjust we shouldn't follow them.

He says that although we're not obligated to eliminate all the bad things in the world, we have an obligation not to participate in them, especially when it comes to the government and the laws the government hands down to the people. Thoreau emphasizes the need to examine laws and see whether or not they hold true to our conscience and moral intuitions. He says that if you know that a specific law is unjust but still decide to act on it, then you're probably not doing the right thing.

Throughout history, government officials who came to the realization that what they were doing was wrong but continued regardless of their moral conscience probably did the wrong thing. The right thing to do, generally speaking, is not to follow unjust laws, rules or orders if they conflict with our most basic moral intuitions. This is what Thoreau called being civilly disobedient. When we disobey unjust laws we're being civilly disobedient, and it is ultimately the right thing to do.

But of course, Thoreau rightly points out that acting against higher authorities is not always easy. Imagine, at a later point in history, a Nazi soldier who decided to betray his allegiance to Hitler and the Nazi regime. Such a person might be risking his own life and the lives of his family. Being civilly disobedient often involves risks. Sometimes they're big risks.

Thoreau himself stopped paying taxes to the American government because he didn't want to support a government that upheld slavery. It was a way of protesting against slavery in America, and as a consequence he spent a night in jail. His actions were ultimately beneficial in playing at least a small part in bringing about the liberation of slaves in America (and he was certainly on the right moral side), but this example illustrates that oftentimes we must take risks. Those risks are ultimately worth it if we're doing the right thing and they further the progression of human civilization.

On Thoreau's account, the disobedient kids in *Stranger Things* would be morally praiseworthy because of their civil disobedience. But where exactly do we see them being civilly disobedient?

Our first clear example is right in the first episode of Season One. As Will, Dustin, and Lucas are riding their bikes back home, Will encounters the monster, which ultimately leads him to go missing. The next day Chief Hopper interrogates Mike, Dustin, and Lucas and they tell him what had happened. They eagerly tell him they want to help look for their friend because they know where he is and how to find him. But Hopper forcefully says, "No. After school, you are all to go home immediately. That means no biking around looking for your friend. Do I make myself clear?"

In this case the boys are faced with a dilemma: obey a proper authority or disobey and try to help their friend. As you know, the boys decide to sneak out at night, hop on their bikes and go to the forest to look for Will. They don't find Will in the forest, but to their surprise they find Eleven, ultimately becoming the primary way they get Will back throughout the season. The boys, in this case, had a strict order imposed on them by an officer of the law but rightly reasoned that it was more important that they use their unique knowledge to help rescue their friend. In this case, the boys were civilly disobedient.

Perhaps the most humorous example of the gang being civilly disobedient comes not at the beginning of the series but right at the end. In the finale of Season Two, everything has been progressing towards finally facing the Mind Flayer along with the other forces that have been holding Will hostage. When Hopper and Joyce Byers are out and about, the boys are at Will's house along with Madmax and Steve Harrington. They were told to stay put because leaving the house could put them in grave danger. Steve Harrington becomes the one in charge of the kids and affirms that staying put is the best thing to do in their situation. Eventually, Billy comes by the house and things get intense. Billy and Steve begin to brawl, leaving Steve unconscious. Madmax then sedates her brother, Billy, by injecting a needle in his neck. Without any viable authority above the gang, they begin to plan their next move. While they know they were told to stay put and not leave the house, they feel the obligation to go help Will by battling the Mind Flayer. They break the rule and steal Billy's car even though none of them know how to drive, throw Steve in the car (still unconscious) and head to their destination. Upon Steve waking he frequently tells them to stop the car but they continue on their way. When they arrive at their destination, Steve attempts to stop them but Dustin replies, "Steve, you're upset, I get it. But the bottom line is, a Party member requires assistance, and it is our duty to provide that assistance." Steve sighs and comes to the realization that they're right, and he decides to help them on their mission. This endeavor ultimately led to successfully saving Will. They could have chosen to stay put, but instead they had the duty to help their friend in need.

It isn't only the kids that are civilly disobedient throughout *Stranger Things*. Chief Hopper himself also often breaks rules in the name of what's right. In Season One, after a search team claims to find Will's body in a local river, Hopper becomes suspicious towards the claim. Hopper suspects that the members of Hawkins Laboratory have planted the body as a cover-up. As the chief, he is definitely aware of the fact that the building has restrictions and high security. Breaking in would imply committing a crime and putting himself in danger. In order to satisfy his reasonable suspicion, however, he decides to go in.

He bypasses some guards by using force, but eventually is successful in his pursuit and finds out that the Hawkins Laboratory lied about Will's body, confirming his suspicion that the body claimed to be Will's was a fake. With the knowledge that the laboratory shouldn't be trusted, he attempts to break in again, this time with Joyce, to find out whether what's causing havoc in the town is coming from the laboratory. This time they get caught and interrogated, but they eventually find out that the laboratory has a portal to the Upside Down realm which has been causing the disarray in the town. Of course, Hopper could have chosen to not break the rules. Instead he decided to be civilly disobedient, leading to him finding out things that ultimately led to Will being saved.

Throughout *Stranger Things* many of the characters are civilly disobedient. They encounter rules and restrictions but are eventually disobey them in order to stay faithful to a higher moral duty. According to Thoreau's point of view, these characters are in the right for the actions that they committed, despite them taking many dangerous risks. Indeed, Thoreau would probably think of them as morally praiseworthy.

Still, if it's true that we have an obligation to be civilly disobedient towards laws that are unjust, we still have the challenge of determining which laws are unjust and shouldn't be followed. To claim that a law is unjust when it isn't could lead to grave consequences, so how do we go about making that determination?

## When Should Laws be Civilly Disobeyed?

Everywhere we go we're confronted by rules and regulations. Our first instinct may be irritation or frustration, or even a mischievous urge to break the rules for the hell of it.

But it's ultimately a good thing to have rules that restrict terrorists, rapists, and other criminals in order for society not to fall into mayhem. Some rules arise objectively from the necessities of living together in comparative peace and harmony. These kinds of restrictions—rules based on what's been called "natural law," as opposed to merely human-constructed rules—become the oil of a properly functioning society, and to the extent that this is so, we have an obligation to follow these kinds of rules.

But does this obligation render *all* rules and restrictions authoritative? Must we always follow every law that higher authorities set in place? Absolutely not! There have been many unjust laws throughout history that were rightly changed by reformers. Progress comes from these social reformers standing up to laws that were unjust and acting against them.

Examples of unjust laws would include laws denying women equality with men or laws restricting inter-racial marriage. Regardless of the reasoning behind these laws, these sorts of laws seem to dehumanize people and so if humans ought to be treated as humans, these would be unjust laws.

In modern life it isn't always easy to identify which laws are just and should be followed and which are unjust and should be disobeyed. When looking at laws throughout history, by contrast, it's often a bit easier to know the answer to this (such as the extremely long time it took for women to be granted the right to vote). Furthermore, we often don't know the consequences that will result from our civil disobedience, which makes the matter even harder. Luckily, the characters from *Stranger Things* provide us with a toolbox of considerations to take into account when analyzing laws and determining whether they're just and should be followed, or unjust and should be rebelled against.

## Laws that Have Bad Intentions Should Be Broken

The first tool for consideration lies in looking at the intent behind a law, rule, or restriction. If a law is put in place in order to conceal things that the public should know, then that could be a cause for concern. Likewise, if the law has as its primary or secondary intention to cause harm based on unfairness, even if it's merely collateral, then that law should probably not be followed. A real-life example of this is bans on immigration for the purposes of not wanting people of other ethnic affiliations—"inferior people"—to enter a country. Note, that laws that restrict immigration for other reasons, such as to preserve a sense of cultural identity or to preserve a workable economy, *may* be just, so here we are focusing solely on a clear racist *intent*.

In *Stranger Things*, an example of this is seen with the Hawkins Laboratory. The laboratory knows a lot of things about the Upside Down that people should know for their own safety. But the Lab keeps the whole thing secret and perpetuates evil as a result. They want to use Eleven for their own benefit. They even conduct various experiments that employ humans as test dummies, which sometimes results in their death. In order to conceal what they know, they develop many rules and restrictions to cover up all the immoral and wrong things they do in the laboratory. These rules are not put in place for society to flourish, but for selfish concerns.

It is right, then, that the kids make frequent attempts to investigate the laboratory. They don't attempt to break in, but they still disobey the rules by operating as spies. If they were a bit older, it's probably safe to say that they would attempt to break into the lab. Chief Hopper, for example, breaks into the lab at least twice in order to find out the truth behind the happenings in the lab, and puts himself in danger. Each time it is morally right for him to do so.

## Laws that Ignore New and Significant Information Should Be Broken

Rules and laws that are set in place are done with a certain presupposed set of knowledge, but because our knowledge is consistently expanding some of our laws will look out of date because of the knowledge gap. A real-life example of this is the historical slave laws in America. These laws restricted African-Americans from being free and living a life they were entitled to. To justify these laws, those in power would often turn to science to justify their laws, often claiming that science had shown that African-Americans were inferior.

One example of this was the theory of *drapetomania*. This theory claimed that an African-American who flees captivity must have a mental illness! While some lawmakers actually believed these pseudoscientific theories, the laws were nonetheless wrong for resting on ignorant notions of racial inequality—and thus it was right to break them. When newer knowledge challenging beliefs in racial inequality emerged, it signaled that the current laws were unjust and helped lead abolitionists to stop slavery. If a law is in conflict with newer, better knowledge then, in most cases, we should probably civilly disobey it.

Throughout *Stranger Things*, this is seen when the laws set in place are ignorant of the Upside Down. In the show, reality consists of an alternate dimension that has negative implications for the dimension we live in. Consequently, the rules that conflict with preserving the well-being of the citizens (like individuals in Hawkins, Indiana) shouldn't be followed. Knowledge of the Upside Down makes some restrictions obsolete. This consideration is not like the first in that is doesn't primarily examine the moral considerations of the law itself. Rather, it looks at the law in light of the facts about the world. And if the law itself does not correspond to the facts then it's probably okay to be civilly disobedient towards it. So, when new and significant knowledge of the world conflicts with certain laws, we don't have the moral obligation to follow them. This does imply that the knowledge can't just be trivial, but it has to be significant enough to justify over-riding the law.

## Laws that Restrict a Greater Good Should Be Broken

Perhaps the best tool or consideration throughout *Stranger Things* to determine whether a law should be broken is whether there is a greater good that can be accomplished in breaking the rule. We don't propose utilitarianism here (where the ends straightforwardly justify the means), but rather that some moral duties seem intuitively more significant than others.

Imagine that you come across an injured individual on the side of a road who is in critical condition. You have to act fast to get that person to the nearest medical center, but there are speeding laws in place in which you can get penalized if you exceed them. If you *don't* go above the limits, you run the risk of *more* harm being inflicted on the individual in critical conditions. Perhaps the right thing to do in this situation is to be as careful as you can and go a reasonable speed, even if it means breaking the speed laws, for the sake of saving the person. In this situation, speed laws aren't wrong in general, but rather they become a barrier to justice, namely, trying to save the person in need. Here the more important moral duty is to try to save a life rather than follow the rules of the road.

In *Stranger Things*, all cases of the kids being morally disobedient seem to be in cases where strong moral duties or considerations—such as rescuing an innocent (Season One) or protecting an entire town from a nefarious evil (Season Two)—outweigh weaker moral concerns, such as disobeying an ignorant authority figure or trespassing.

## Do the Right Thing

There have been individuals, such as terrorists, who have claimed to be civilly disobedient but have really committed atrocious acts in a grotesque and unjustified way. It's easy, given a limited perspective, to think of a just law being unjust or an unjust law being just. Because of this we need tools to determine which laws ought to be obeyed and which laws it's right ton disobey.

With these examples from *Stranger Things*, we've only begun to scratch the surface. These "tools" are not exhaustive nor are they necessarily infallible. They're not meant to be misused in order to justify unjust rebellion against society. But they are a start; they are there to help us decide when we should be civilly disobedient.

For the most part, rules should be followed. They are most often set in place to keep things orderly and for society to flourish. However, when rules are unjust, fight against the greater good, or ignore new knowledge, civil disobedience is needed to reform and change rules, in order for human progress to occur.

And so, if we want to do what's right, we can look to the examples of Mike, Dustin, Lucas, Will, Madmax, and Hopper for inspiration.

# 14
# Friends Don't Lie

COLE BOWMAN

"Friends don't lie." Mike Wheeler's words resound through Hawkins, repeating through his group of comrades as they live through the terror taking over the small town. From the very beginning, *Stranger Things* has been a study of human relationships and nowhere is this more apparent than in the friendships between the young characters of Hawkins as they face the horrors that unfold.

The ways that they approach their friendships define not only their development as people but also the nature of the world that surrounds them. Again and again, they discuss the true nature of friendship while teaching Eleven and confronting challenges that threaten to destroy them.

Mike has taken it upon himself to teach Eleven (the strange girl who escaped from the menacing research laboratory at the edge of town) what it means to be a friend when she joins up with his group. On the one hand, this noble pursuit is immediately endearing and we all want Mike and the gang to share the merits of their friendship with the Eggo-obsessed girl. Simultaneously it runs the risk of producing some troubling outcomes, as the consequences of friendship, of course, are much more than they may seem at the outset. In an area filled with potential people to teach her the nature of friendship, is Mike Wheeler really the right person to be doing so?

# On a Curiosity Voyage

To figure out the value of Mike's friendship, we must first understand what "friendship" means in the first place. The nature of friendship seems like something that should be intuitive in all of us, but the topic of what makes a "good friendship" has been notoriously troublesome in philosophical literature.

Philosophical all-star Aristotle (384–322 B.C.E.) is traditionally at the center of most debates about friendship because of his landmark work *Ethics*. He's talked about for good reason because, along with his establishment of one of the most well-respected ethical systems, *virtue ethics*, Aristotle managed to whip up a model for the ideal kinds of friendships in the same work. In his book *Nicomachean Ethics*, he neatly divvies up the various "categories" of friendship into a hierarchy:

- **friendship of pleasure**
- **friendship of utility**
- **friendship of virtue**

Given that you know that Aristotle's ethical system is called "virtue ethics," it's probably not a surprise that Aristotle thought that friendships of virtue are the ideal.

Friendships of pleasure are found in the everyday kinds of friendliness that we see permeating through our normal lives. There's not merely one single kind of friendship of pleasure, but they are the most shallow kind, as far as Aristotle's concerned. They can range from the simple social politeness we treat each other with to the kind that are found through mutual enjoyment of one another.

This is the sort of friendliness that Mrs. Wheeler treated Joyce Byers with by bringing her a casserole after Will's disappearance. This is also what seems to drive several aspects of what becomes known as "The Party" in Hawkins's Middle School. That is, of course, comprised of Mike Wheeler, Will Byers, Lucas Sinclair, and Dustin Henderson.

While The Party as a whole is something we'll touch on later, there are certain aspects of the group that Aristotle would declaim as his lowest order of friendship. Early on in the series, this appears to be the nature of Dustin and

Lucas's friendship. While the relationship between them develops over the course of time, it's clear in the beginning of the series that the two boys spend time together mostly because of their shared interests. They both like playing Dungeons & Dragons, they both like action figures, bike riding, and comic books. Lucas and Dustin, as it becomes clear in at the end of Season One, however, are not the best of friends in even their own friend group, let alone in the series. In fact, their relationship is such an ideal fit with the nature of the friendship of pleasure at the beginning of the show that they even help to illustrate the problems that Aristotle saw with this dynamic.

The two spend time with each other out of convenience and mutual pleasures, but when the going gets tough, their relationship starts to fall apart and hostilities rise. Probably the most memorable scene that comes to mind when considering their sometimes fraught dynamic occurs in Season Two when the extra-cool new girl Max moves to the school. Both enamored by the red headed "zoomer," they begin to blame the other for their own problems when faced by the prospect of competing with one another for her attention. This dynamic is almost exactly what Aristotle worries about when it comes to the friendship of pleasure. To Aristotle, the fact that the boys begin to quarrel is a firm testament to the flimsiness of the friendship of pleasure.

## Useful Friends

In contrast to the friendship of pleasure, the friendship of utility is the kind of relationship that serves a useful function in the lives of the people involved. During Season One, this sort of friendship is at the core of Nancy Wheeler and Jonathan Byers's involvements with one another. While it's quite clear in the first place that Jonathan has a (rather creepy) crush on Nancy, their friendship is squared firmly in the realm of utility as they investigate the disappearances of Nancy's friend Barbara and Jonathan's little brother, Will.

Their usefulness to one another is the basis for their otherwise unlikely friendship, spurring them to spend time with one another even after Nancy finds out that Jonathan took pictures of her undressing at Steve's house. It's not every day that you have someone who can sympathize with you about your loved one disappearing at the hands of a Demogorgon, after all! Both are the only people outside of Hawkins's lab that know about the creature for several episodes and their friendship grows while they search for clues to the whereabouts of their loved ones.

Much like Dustin and Lucas, their friendship changes over the course of their time together, and once their utility to one another ends during Season One the basis of their friendship must as well. Nancy makes a note midway through Season Two that there was an estrangement between them after Will's reappearance that she couldn't quite reconcile. The problem with the friendship of utility is very similar to that of pleasure: when the utility has been spent from the relationship, it falls apart. In the case of the pair of older siblings, their friendship hits a head when their goal is met. At the end of Season One they've both learned the nature of the Upside Down and recovered Will, and their friendship begins to disassemble. The first episode of Season Two makes it clear that, while the two of them are still spending time together, their dynamic has changed considerably. As the season continues, their position with each other vacillates in uncertainty as they're not entirely sure where they stand with one another. Aristotle wouldn't be surprised to learn that, once their usefulness to one another ends, they must renegotiate their friendship. In this case, it's replaced by an alienating awkwardness and eventually a romantic relationship.

## Virtuous Friends

Luckily for Hawkins, not all of Aristotle's orders of friendship are quite as shallow as these two. For Aristotle, what's left in the wake of these rather unsatisfying friendship dynamics is the ideal: a friendship of *virtue*. As mentioned before, Aristotle's entire ethical paradigm hinges on the idea of virtue, so the friendship of virtue is a natural result of this kind of moral setup. The reason for this being that *every* aspect of your life should be making you a better (more virtuous) person, so your friends should be the people who nurture goodness in you.

While this seems like a one-in-million kind of friendship on the face of it, the virtuous friendship is much more common than you might think. Part of the reason that a virtuous friendship is hard to see—even when it's right in front of you—is that it's subtle. One potential friendship of virtue in *Stranger Things* is in everyone's favorite Demogorgon victim, Barbara Holland. Even though she's only in a whopping seven episodes (even when you include photographs of her and scenes that feature her dead body), Barbara made quite the impression on the audience. Perhaps the ineffability of why such a minor character elicited such a strong reception of fans of the show was the simple quality of friendship found in her relationship to Nancy.

Barbara meets her untimely demise in "Holly, Jolly," after she's taken by the Demogorgon during Steve Harrington's party. The reason she's sitting poolside with a bloody hand: her best friend Nancy Wheeler asked her to keep an eye on her at the party. She says in the previous episode ("The Weirdo on Maple Street"): "You can be, like, my guardian. All right? Make sure I don't get drunk and do anything stupid." Even after Nancy makes it clear that she's changed her mind and wants to stay the night with Steve (which is not in question here—people are allowed to change their minds about things), Barb hangs around to make sure that she's safe. The fact that this scene is the part of the show that leads to Barb's death is bitter, but the fact that she fulfills her promise to her friend is not. In fact, this level of attention toward Nancy's safety is likely why Nancy is compelled to find her justice. Not only was Barb a friend, she was a *good* friend according to Aristotle.

If something doesn't feel quite right when looking at this moment as evidence of a friendship of virtue, it is because of one small but important difference between virtuous friendships: they don't have to be equal. In fact, this dynamic points out that Aristotle's categories of friendship are hard to pin down because Aristotle recognized that friendships have *directionality*. What this means is that, at any point in time, the people in a friendship can be operating on two different orders of Aristotelian friendship. This is obviously a source of a lot of grief for people even inside of Hawkins. We see this uneven type of relationship between Tommy H.

and Steve in the First Season, where Steve wants a friendly relationship of pleasure and Tommy H. is trying to utilize Steve as a social climber. This is one of the (many) reasons that their friendship ultimately fails.

The true beauty of the virtuous friendship is that it's not really folly to these directional failures. If person A is a really good friend to person B and helps them become a better, more moral person, the friendship itself is considered virtuous. Even if person B isn't reciprocating, the very action of helping someone be a better person is a moral good. Because person A is helping person B be, let's say, more honest, then person A is getting a little bit of a moral kickback from their own for having helped them. One of the awesome things about a virtuous friendship is that, even if the ideal mutual virtue isn't available there is an unselfishness to the whole setup.

## Teaching Virtue

This brings us back to our original question: is Mike Wheeler really the person to be teaching Eleven the virtues of friendship? Is Mike Wheeler a virtuous friend to Eleven? The answer to this question can only be complicated because he both *is* and *is not* a virtuous friend to Eleven. He invests deeply in her well-being, concealing her from his parents and the authorities in order to keep her safe, all while providing her with the sort of nurturing friendship we should aspire to at times. At other times, he blames her involving them with the whole business of the Upside Down, accuses her of lying to them about Will's death, and exploits her powers. In order to fairly examine their relationship, the budding romantic tension between them also can't be ignored. In this light, the only thing we can really say is that Mike Wheeler is indeed often a virtuous friend to Eleven, but certainly not always. This unsatisfying conclusion highlights one of the major problems with this paradigm of friendship as it defies one of the basic parts of the human experience: *the ability to change*.

Though Aristotle believed that you could move between these categories (ideally toward a more virtuous friendship), he doesn't account much for the everyday shifts that happen in a complex friend group like what we see in our intrepid

Dungeons & Dragons–playing Party. In any given chapter, at least one member of the group (usually Mike) is in conflict with one of the others. Mike and Lucas fight over whether or not the former should be helping Eleven; Dustin and Lucas fight over the extent to which they're helping the search for Will.; Eleven and Mike fight over her changing the compass readings; and Mike resents Lucas and Dustin for inviting Max to trick-or-treat with them on Halloween.

Sure, all of them eventually reconcile, but this isn't something that should be overlooked just because it ends up okay. This kind of constant shifting of grounds is important, because it makes us take a little bit of a more complex stand on the issue of friendship in Hawkins, Indiana. If the friendships are constantly shifting, how can this sort of categorization effectively show their standing? Luckily for us, later philosophers did away with this sort of categorization altogether.

## Why Don't You Have Any Friends?

Friedrich Nietzsche had a lot of different ideas about friendship from his predecessor's, even though he does cite Aristotle in much of his own work. While Nietzsche laid many of his philosophical foundations in the same groundwork of the ancient Greeks, his concept of friendship is significantly more targeted than is Aristotle's.

For one, Nietzsche makes an explicit differentiation between "friend" and the person being "befriended," rather than just the implied directionality in virtue ethics. This dynamic is one of the key reasons why Nietzsche's work is of interest to us—it accounts for all of those subtle changes that undermine Aristotle's system. We're not asking whether Eleven is capable of being a good friend just yet (she's just learning), but we're very interested in whether or not the rest of the people in Hawkins are being good friends *to* her. So, for our purposes, consider Eleven as the "befriended" and everyone else as the "friend."

Nietzsche's main principle of friendship is both similar to and very different from Aristotle's virtuous friendship. The similarity lies in Nietzsche's belief that the friendships we foster should help to cultivate all of our personal potential, much like Aristotle's call for virtuous nurturing. The difference is that Nietzsche believed that the nature of our friendships shouldn't rely on abstract ideals (like Aristotle's virtues), but real world situations.

In his book *Human, All Too Human* (1878), Nietzsche stresses the importance of looking at the human experience through the lens of our most basic nature: *the human animal*. In order to live as well as we possibly can, we must keep our nature grounded in the very animality of our needs. Against abstract idealization, Nietzsche believes that our constant strivings for perfect states or abstracted ideas is one of the things that misguides our actions and morality in life. Aristotle's virtues of honesty and courage and all that? Nietzsche thinks we're deluding ourselves in thinking that we can ever reach such lofty goals. Instead, we ought to spend our time trying to live our lives as greatly as possible. In terms that even Mad Max would approve of, Nietzsche thinks we should do everything we can to not be a total wasteoid.

So, what does this have to do with friendship? Nietzsche's concept of friendship is based in this "natural state" of humanity, in which our friends are those people who challenge us to live our best possible lives. The *way* that Nietzsche suggests others should challenge us to live our best lives is to be those people who actually *challenge* us to do so. Through conflict. Probably Nietzsche's most famous quote is the incredible: "Whatever doesn't kill me makes me stronger." *This* is the sort of thing he's talking about there. Your friends will make you stronger by trying to, well, not kill you . . . but maybe by fighting you a bit.

Remember Aristotle's feelings about Dustin and Lucas? Where Aristotle thought that the two of them weren't ideal friends because of their many conflicts, Nietzsche believes that the conflicts are what make them great friends. By the end of Season Two, the two boys had made their way to the other side of their conflict and became the best of friends again. And to top it off, they treat each other far better than they did before they'd aired out some of their problems.

One such telling moment between Lucas and Dustin comes about in "The Spy" when, after lying to the rest of the Party about his demodog "pet," D'artagnon (Dart), Dustin admits the truth to Lucas that he'd kept Dart hidden. Had Lucas not challenged him earlier on in the episode, had he not *confronted* him about the danger his lie could have exposed them all to, Dustin wouldn't have learned valuable information about the nature of the creature he'd stumbled upon and about the responsibility one has for cleaning up after mistakes. This event doesn't happen in a vacuum, either, as they struggle with each other several times throughout the two seasons, but in this struggle they are each made better for it. To Nietzsche, Dustin and Lucas's friendship is the ideal model of how a friendship should operate.

On a similar note, Lucas has thereby been integral to Eleven's development in a Nietzschean sense. During Season One in particular, the tension between Lucas and Eleven is a constant source of strife within the Party with them coming to a particularly violent boiling point in Chapter 5 when she uses her powers to throw him across a junkyard after he and Mike get into an argument about her. This conflict has several outcomes for the Party: it shows El that she needs to be wary of manipulating people (friends don't lie), it reinforces the bond between Lucas and Dustin (when the letter defends him to Mike), and it forces Mike to re-evaluate the priorities that he has between his friends. Most importantly, Lucas challenging Eleven teaches her that she shouldn't be so open with using her powers on other people. By being willing to confront her for her behavior, Lucas, not Mike, is a much better friend to Eleven in a Nietzschean sense.

## She's Our Friend and She's Crazy!

Not satisfied with Nietzsche? Worried this kind of thinking might lead to a miserable life full of conflict? Sure, there's a great deal of good to be found in a person who'll keep you in check when you're going all haywire with your psychic powers, but there has to be some other option for how a good friendship works. One that's not too abstract or too challenging?

You're not alone in your concern. More recent philosophers have worried about the same exact thing. Two such thinkers, Carol Gilligan and Nel Noddings are among them.

They're also two of the philosophers responsible for founding a field of thought called "the ethics of care." The basic idea of the ethics of care (or "care ethics", pick whichever you like) is that the relationships that we form are what make us into the people that we are.

Much like both Aristotle and Nietzsche, care ethicists believe that our friendships should nurture the goodness in us. Unlike both of them, though, care ethicists don't find much value in trying to lay out a strict set of rules for how we should engage with out friends so long as the methods that we use to approach these relationships put the care of another as the top priority.

In care ethics, there are two basic "positions" in a relationship dynamic, which include the "one-caring" and the "cared-for." In many cases, this dynamic remains directional like Aristotle's and Nietzsche's approaches do, but the best-case scenario is for a mutual relationship in which both people are the "one-caring" *and* the "cared-for." What's even more amazing about care ethics is that the respect the system poses for a two-friend relationship can also be extended to a group, so long as the dynamic can support all of the individuals present in it.

*This* is the real secret to the friendships of Hawkins Middle school: the Party. The ethics of care urges us to look at this group as a whole, and not just because of the old Dungeons & Dragons adage to "never split the party." Where each of the individuals in the party has their own setbacks and their own things to offer, the Party as a whole is responsible for each of its constituent parts. From each of the original four (Mike, Will, Lucas and Dustin) to all of the others they've collected along the way (Eleven, Max, and Steve).

The foundation of the friendship that holds together the Party is that they all care about each other. That's nowhere more evident than in Mike's, Dustin's, and Lucas's dogged fight about what happened to Will when he went missing. Though there were *compelling* reasons why they shouldn't involve themselves in the search for Will (the danger involved, the social pressures to keep everything under wraps, and the fact that Hopper explicitly told them not to), they never give up on their friend. Even when they've been presented with a grim simulacrum of him bobbing in the water in the quarry, one slim piece of evidence keeps them searching. It's this care that makes their connection so powerful.

So, the ethics of care's beautiful answer to this question of whether or not Mike is the right person to be teaching Eleven about friendship is yes, he is, but he isn't acting alone. Eleven is learning about friendship not just from Mike Wheeler, but the rest of the Party as well. Where any one of them fails, the others can make up for the differences so that the needs of all can be met. Mike teaches her lofty moral ideas about truth, Dustin teaches her not to take her clothes off in front of them all, and Lucas challenges her desire to use her powers on them all. The nature of friendship is unfolding around her and, while she's something of a blank slate for how relationships work, she's taking an accelerated course from the boys. Because they care about each other, they are the exact right people to be teaching her what friendship means.

## Democracy and Demogorgons

Since we've determined the group of friends that Eleven was inducted into, the Party, is quite good for her, the last thing we need to settle is why any of this is important. While, sure, we should care about her wellbeing (just as Gilligan and Noddings said we should), French philosopher Jacques Derrida can help us understand why it's critical for a girl with trans-dimensional super powers to have a good foundation of friendship.

In *The Politics of Friendship*, Derrida concludes that all of politics, and any other real social organization, is just an extrapolation upon the basic relationships that exist in our ordinary lives. Democracy itself lays its roots in the relationships of the everyday person, much like the Upside Down does in the Hawkins Laboratory basement. According to Derrida, "Democracy means, minimally, equality—and here you see why friendship is an important key, because in friendship, even in classical friendship, what is involved is reciprocity, equality, symmetry."

This is why Derrida would insist that The Party was on the right track, friendship-wise. The group insists on a democratic basis in which they are all equal, where each can contribute to the care of the others and all of them can be cared for by the group. This shares a lot of the same basic elements with the ethics of care, sure, but his standpoint insists on one additional dimension that makes a huge difference: Derrida believes that the way we treat our friends is the way that we engage with the world as a whole. We learn the "rules" for being a part of society from our friendships because Derrida believes that friendship is the foundation for society itself. So, Eleven being treated with care and equity by the group teaches her how to care for other people as she tries to become part of dangerous world outside of Hawkins Laboratory.

Derrida's approach to friendship sets the stakes pretty high for the kids of Hawkins, but maybe we shouldn't take this sort of thing lightly. Fundamentally, how we treat our friends is at the core of how we treat the world at large. Nowhere is this more evident than when Eleven repeats Mike's words to other people in her life: "Friends don't lie." She says this to Hopper, to Kali, and to Mike himself. Beyond just that, Eleven's friendships back in Hawkins are the reason she knows that she's being exploited by Kali and her group when she runs away. Her friends are the reason she goes back to Indiana and closes the gate to the Upside Down.

## When Your Friends Are Upside Down

The distressing thing about the nature of friendship in Hawkins is its ties to the otherworldly physics of the Upside Down. While the truth of the area is still questionable, the series has hinted significantly at a paranormal connection between El and the Upside Down. Even if she isn't the monster that she (and Lucas) are afraid she is, the stakes for her friendships are high because she's a remarkable girl who can move things with her brain. (The extent of her powers is still as yet unknown—she might be able to do much more than fend off the Mind Flayer.) Regardless of how cool it is to think about her powers, the fact that she has them at all makes her dangerous.

Had Eleven been found by someone else, say someone like Billy or Troy, both notorious bullies, what would she have learned about the lessons of friendship? Would she learn that it was fun to make ridicule someone because of his missing teeth? To terrorize younger kids by trying to run them over with a sports car? We don't need to look too far to see what can happen if Eleven falls in with the wrong crowd. The very first scene of Season Two introduces Kali (Eight), another one of the children experimented on by Dr. Brenner. Eleven's foray in the "big city" with Kali gives us some idea of what might have happened, as she almost became a vigilante killer, using her powers to track people down and destroy them. In fact, it's the memory of her friends that spurs Eleven to leave that kind of violence and Kali's crew behind to go back to Hawkins.

The friends that Eleven makes play a significant role in who she becomes and in what becomes of her ethical standpoint. Much like the magnetic field being generated by Hawkins Lab, her friends guide her *moral* compass. Perhaps, if he'd had some better friends, Dr. Brenner wouldn't be such a self-aggrandizing, creepy, murderous waisteoid. Maybe if Kali had some better friends, she wouldn't be so willing to treat the world with such unflinching cruelty. Perhaps, as the case may be, Eleven won't be willing to use her powers to hurt and manipulate others precisely *because* she has such good friends.

# 15
# Abnormal Is the New Normal

FERNANDO GABRIEL PAGNONI BERNS,
DIEGO FORONDA, AND MARIANA ZÁRATE

Stylistically, *Stranger Things* is all about the Eighties: the fonts, the hairdos, the clothes, and the general feeling. The same goes for the main narrative: kids in peril, extraordinary children with paranormal powers (so Spielberg!), evil conspiracies, and the Stephen King vibe. Ideologically, however . . . the TV series is not completely 1980s. And that's a *very* good thing.

Even if this hit TV show feels like the 1980s, we must accept the truth: it is a binge show that recreates a time where nobody even knows what a "binge show" could mean. The show has been developed in a new scenario completely alien to Ronald Reagan's era. Unlike the real 1980s, millennial *Stranger Things* plays with a fresh, multicultural point of view that emphasizes diversity and ways of being *not* normal. The characters use a millennial voice packaged in 1980s aesthetics.

*Stranger Things* should be read *anachronically*—being aware that some attitudes, situations, or facts do not belong to the correct historical or chronological time. Only through the anachronisms scattered throughout the show can audiences see the core of the series: normalcy is not a given thing—a "natural" thing—but a social discourse, something that changes from era to era and culture to culture. The anachronical nature of *Strangers Things* allows those of us in the United States, viewers in the new millennium, to experience how different our current sense of American normalcy is in contrast with that of the real 1980s.

Anachronisms produce the interruption of history as an oversimplified temporal line that goes from A to B. The anachronism is a countertime that explains how certain events and thinking may be understood by a present-day viewer. As philosopher Georges Didi-Huberman explains, our reading of visual media is anachronical: we read and explore images of the past with new mentalities that allows us to engage critically with these images.

How does anachronism help us understand freakiness and the politics of normalcy? According to Michel Foucault, *normalcy* is a social construct which establishes a hierarchy that judges everything "normal" as being "superior" to the abnormal, considered "inferior." Foucault argued that the power of hegemonic thinking lies in its ability to create new subjects, or "freaks" such as nerds, homosexuals, or tomboys. These "inferior" abnormal subjects are oppressed through social discourses such as the ridicule that the kids' heroes of *Stranger Things* must endure by their "normal" bully tormentors.

These mechanisms of control—and labeling someone a freak *is* a form of control—can only be explored when we understand that *Stranger Things* is, by nature, an anachronism: what was abnormal at the 1980s, is proud identity now.

## The 1980s Are So In!

To Georges Didi-Huberman, confronting the image implies the confrontation with time. Not just the time within the image—such as the time unfolding within a movie—but the chronological time: each work of art speaks about its time, its context of production. When a viewer sees a film, she is also watching the time of its production: a black and white film provides us with information about the stars of the era, the dress codes, customs, behavior, ways of acting, and types of corporeal beauty.

*Stranger Things* tries to reproduce, without fissures, a time long past. After a short prologue where a sweaty scientist is devoured by an unseen beast, "The Vanishing of Will Byers" opens with four friends—Will, Mike, Dustin and Lucas—playing a board game in a furnished basement within a typical house within a typical suburban landscape. The posters covering the walls speak about John Carpenter's

*The Thing*, everyone wears T-shirts and hats that scream "1980s!" Most of the women of the show wear the huge hairdos beloved of that decade. Parents even fight with enormous TV apparatuses with huge impractical antennas that never seem to catch good reception. The recreation of the time is perfect, at least, visually.

There is another implication about time, however. The work of art also contains an *ideological* time. Each image also speaks to us of the ways in which a given culture and society represented itself.

We can take an archaeological approach to art. We cannot escape to the anachronical view when watching *Stranger Things*: we now find ridiculous the vision of women fainting rather than fighting back in horror movies because we see these works of the past with contemporary eyes. We all cheer that both Joyce Byers and Nancy Wheeler—just to name two examples—are resilient and can investigate. In the 1980s, these empowered women would have relied, at some point, on men. Here, they are examples of women with agencies of their own.

Classical historiography and the equally classic idea that the past must be analyzed with objectivity propose that the investigator must push aside any trace of subjectivity. In classical historiography, art rests on chronological time; each stage in the history of art is thought to be improved by another stage, better than the previous one.

But history is also made of personal memories, so the investigator should not drop subjectivity, but embrace it as part of her investigation. The science of the past ought to be studied with all the knowledge and analytical tools that we have today. This approach will help us to understand how our society developed through the years. Investigating the past with our contemporary eyes and tools, however, means falling into anachronism—interpreting the past with contemporary categories. Anachronism may be an error, but it may sometimes turn out that anachronism is a good tool. We should sometimes celebrate anachronisms rather than avoid them.

## Clash of the Eras

The disruption of time presented through *Stranger Things* illuminates both the era and the way of thinking during the

1980s. This clash of time-periods, reading the 1980s through a contemporary lens, is what makes the show so rich for interpretation. Unlike the real and highly normative 1980s, *Stranger Things* celebrates freakiness and difference in today's terms.

In the first episode of Season One ("The Vanishing of Will Byers"), Will appropriately disappears. His mother Joyce asks the cops to find her son. Through her nervous rambling, she calls her son delicate and addresses the fact that other kids call Will a fag and a queer. Chief Jim Hopper asks Joyce if Will is indeed gay. Joyce defends her son when she rightly states that Will's sexuality has no relationship with his disappearance.

In this scene, Joyce does not behave as a 1980s mother *at all!* It's unlikely that a mother in that decade would let pass the suggestion that her son is gay. Most 1980s mothers would indignantly defend their own sons' heterosexuality: "How dare you? My son is normal!" To Joyce, however, her son's sexuality is of little importance. Joyce is acting as a modern mother. *Stranger Things* is a show made in the new millennium and shaped by millennial sensibilities where the collective LGBTQIA+ community more often makes itself visible in a world that is slowly (maybe a little *too slowly*) accepting difference.

In Season Two Jonathan Byers claims his right to be called a freak. He is assuming a role that very few teenagers in the 1980s would be proud of. The 1980s were years of conservatism and normalization after the progressive 1970s, a decade which, for many, had set the United States on the wrong track. A lot of movies in the 1980s were led by nerds, shy guys, or freaks, but every one of them wanted the same thing: *normalcy*. Probably, a very small number of adolescents during those years were proclaiming their right to be different the way Jonathan and Will do in the first season of *Stranger Things*. After all, being different was a bad thing, an inability to fit in.

But nobody screams "anachronism!" louder than poor Barb, who surpassed the expectations usually awarded to such a minor character. Barb was the typical "canon fodder" of any horror film: she does not fit into normal conceptions of beauty and was, basically, a secondary character. Someone must die first, right? Soon enough, Barbara was killed by the monstrous Demogorgon ("Holly, Jolly"). Her murder, however, caused an unusual response from viewers who strongly identified with her as a shy girl and a warm friend. Mass identification with a plain and awkward character! What kind of world are we living in?

Basically, we're living in the new millennium and Barb allowed viewers to identify with her sense of friendship and alternative ways of being. She embodied a different type of adolescence and femininity than what many viewers find charming, so her death was cause for concern and sorrow. In the 1980s the movie death of a character like Barb would be barely noticed, as viewers mostly identified with the popular blonde girls and the chaste but gorgeous heroine.

These anachronisms appear throughout *Stranger Things*, pointing to two interrelated issues: first, that leaving all the reconstructed spirit of an era aside, the show is made with the care for celebrating difference. Second, and most important, all these anachronisms reveal that normalcy is fluid and changes from time to time. What was abnormal in the 1980s, is now considered just a way of life—if even noticed at all.

## Freaks and Geeks

Normalcy in the 1980s mostly meant fitting within unabashed white middle-class materialism. After two decades of excesses—the 1960s and the 1970s—which gave visibility to previously ignored collectives such as the LGBTQIA+, black, feminist, or Latinx communities, the Reagan era came to enthrone family values and traditional thinking. Being different was considered deeply problematic. Sitcoms projecting "family values" returned with full force in harmony with the conservative climate of the Reagan years. Happy families with cute kids and a pet populated TV shows and, supposedly, the real world.

Coding someone as "abnormal" is a way of bringing that person under the punitive gaze of power. Thus, anything that could escape the status quo—the vision of the world sustained by those who hold the power in a given society in a given historical moment—could be declared "abnormal" and, in consequence, sick, evil, or deviant. The normal and the abnormal were constituted as explanatory categories of goodness and badness.

In this sense, the whole first season of *Stranger Things* is based on the cruel relationship that Eleven has with Martin Brenner, her father figure. In "Holly, Jolly," Brenner puts Eleven in solitary confinement since she refused to telekinetically harm a cat. Since she has disobeyed "Daddy," he punishes her. Supposedly, he wants her to control her powers so she can be normal. What Brenner wants, in fact, is to gain complete control of Eleven and use the little girl as a military weapon. He pursues his plans, creating a scenario where he is the good guy and she is the monster that must be controlled.

French philosopher Michel Foucault dedicated his life to the analysis of how society and the State exert power over people through the encoding of the abnormal. The organization of power over life, according to Foucault, is based on anatomical and individual policies centered on the body and punishment. Any individual who commits a crime must receive a horrid punishment upon his or her body. As the world progresses, however, Foucault noticed a shift in the ways of maintaining control: the rise of biopolitics, meaning a regulation of the entire population through discipline (rather than just individual corporeal punishment). This discipline comes with the notion of the abnormal as the person who behaves in a way not sanctioned by society.

Foucault sees power being exerted over society by the law and by medicine, each of which claims a certain type of knowledge. The power exerted by judges and doctors is the power of *normalization*, the power to label individuals as abnormal. Foucault sees the roots of the abnormal in figures that preceded it: the *monster*, the *individual to be corrected*, and the *masturbator*.

## The Monster

The monster transgresses the law and represents not only a violation of society, but of nature as well. The monster is both an extreme phenomenon and an extremely rare one; it is exception. The monster is thought of as a hybrid creature shaped by the cohabitation of a mixture of forms. The Demogorgon is the perfect example of the prototypical rare monster.

Foucault found that the sexually androgynous body was, historically, one of the privileged forms of monstrosity. Accordingly, Troy, the bully tormenting the main group of friends, maintains that Eleven's chief monstrous trait is to be a girl who looks like a boy. A transgression of the "natural" limits and a transgression of any system of classifications: this is what constitutes the monster.

Eleven's appearance in the first season codes her as a "tomboy," a girl who enjoys participating in activities that are supposedly natural for boys and who has little interest in ordinarily feminine things such as make-up or clothes. The tomboy demarcates the limits of acceptable forms of girlhood; she is a figure often accepted in society because she, as the years go by, will discard her masculine appearance to become a normal woman (the fact that she discards the masculine traits in Season Two indicates that she has a preference to not be masculine). If the tomboy does not become a true woman, there is no need to worry, as the discipline exerted upon her by social pressure will oblige her to fall in line.

Eleven is a person but without a proper name: she is called a number, a label that turns her into a thing. Eleven's incarnation as a monster is the title of the sixth episode of Season One, "The Monster," and she even calls herself that when she says: "The gate. I opened it. I'm the monster." When Eleven disappears, Lucas tells Mike: "We're looking for some stupid monster but did you ever stop to think that maybe she's the monster?"

## Corrected Individuals

The second figure identified by Foucault, the so-called "individual to be corrected," is more frequent and more temporally close to us than the monster. If the monster is the exception, the "individual to be corrected" is common. Unlike the monster, inextricably linked to nature, the individual to be corrected "emerges in the play of relations of conflict and support that exist between the family and the school, workshop, street, quarter, parish, church, police, and so on" (*Abnormal*, pp. 57–58). Rather than being an abomination, like the monster, the individual to be corrected is linked to social institutions such as schools and families. These social institutions are those in charge of keeping the individual on track or, even better, "corrected."

Terry Ives, Eleven's mother, is an example of the individual to be corrected. She was a hippie, a figure strongly linked with insurrection in the 1960s. Thus, Eleven's monstrosity is linked to her mother's incorrect behavior. Furthermore, Terry was linked to experimentation with LSD, a psychedelic drug used by hippie culture and by the government. The use of drugs enhances the violation of the norm and is presented as the origin of the sins of abnormality that will continue on in her daughter Eleven.

Correction assumes norms, and norms are fluid. What has to be corrected in prior times may now be considered legitimate. Joyce, as a divorced mother, is put under the microscope and all her seemingly irrational behaviors in Season One and her worries in Season Two are examined in terms of female hysteria or hypersensibility. She is the prototype of the "crazy" woman who lives with kids but not husband who can correct her. After all, there was a conventional wisdom claiming that women are essentially psychologically fragile and thus, prone to emotional imbalance. Throughout Season One, the entire town offers Joyce their condolences while asking her to calm down. What for the town is maternal hysteria, for Joyce is determination to find her son.

Even Mike, Lucas, Will, and Dustin need to be corrected. They need to "man up," embrace the "right" things to do for boys, like sports, rather than play in the basement. The bullies tormenting them, in turn, behave like "normal" boys: they are aggressive. That is why no adult punishes them: they do what boys do. Being aggressive means being "macho," rightfully manly. Mike, Lucas, Will, and Dustin are those who are in the wrong here, in the macho 1980s.

## The Masturbator

The third figure seems to be the more enigmatic: the masturbator. How can this figure lead to the abnormal? What interests Foucault is the fact that the masturbator's field is something even more intimate than the family: his frame of reference is no longer nature (the monster) and society (the individual to be corrected), but the bedroom, the bed, the body. Thus, politics of State intervention and social correction filter the most intimate of spaces. The supervisors are the family, the doctors, and the Church. Even imagination is put under surveillance. The control is now complete since all institutions would correct you and tell how behave and what to think, in order to be considered normal. Even if nobody is watching you when home alone, you have the rules so internalized within your psyche that you behave "properly."

## Strange and Abnormal

The abnormal is the descendant of these three individuals. The abnormal will be policed through discipline, normalization, and biopolitics. *Biopolitics* is the intervention of social and cultural politics within the bodies of populations (rather than individuals). Biopolitics optimizes a standard state of life; everyone that separates from the normative way of life, will be oppressed through institutions (such as the asylum or jail) or, simply put, actions such as public ridicule and humiliation, until the person discards difference and embraces "normality."

In *Stranger Things*, the abnormality is embodied in several of the characters and reveals how historically grounded the abnormal is. Troy identifies each member of the "freak show" by nicknaming them with terms that, now in the new millennium, can be classified as politically incorrect but were more freely used in the 1980s. Since he is black, Lucas is nicknamed "Midnight." Dustin is named "Toothless," despite the fact that he clarifies that his medical condition has the medical name of "cleydocranial dysplasia." Mike is called "Frogface" because of the shape of his face. Will is simply called "queer," a term which was extremely pejorative and painful in previous decades. In recent years, the LGBTQIA+ community claimed the term "queer" as an umbrella definition that avoids oversimplification at the moment of labeling sexualities. Philosophers and scholars alike took the term "queer" and turned it into a new discipline of investigation, revealing a shift from abnormality—the queer as a homosexual monster—to the academic.

Still, nobody is queerer than Eleven, called "freak" because "her head is shaved. She doesn't even look like a girl"

("The Bathtub"). She looks androgynous, neither male nor female. We can find here another interesting anachronism linked to abnormality. Before singer Sinead O'Connor put shaved heads in vogue during the 1990s, extremely short hair on girls and women was considered a signpost of the abnormal, butch, or a lack or failure to attain proper femininity.

The failure of Eleven in all rites of sociability makes her a weirdo. She is different, especially for the norms of the 1980s. Lucas and Dustin think, at first, that she is a fugitive from an asylum; thus, "she's probably a psycho" ("The Weirdo on Maple Street"). Mental illness, rather than a condition, was linked to freakiness and evilness. In the same episode, Lucas predicts that she "will be back in the loony bin."

The "loony bin" is part of the systems of discipline. The State must confine the abnormal to a space of rectification. But the recurrent bullying exerted by Troy and his group of friends is also a form of discipline encouraged by the State. Recurrent ridicule obliges people to behave the way society expects them to do. The State sanctions the bullies' behavior because the bullies and their cruel ways are the normal; they behave as normal kids should, mocking their weak class-mates. Schools were not even *that* worried about bullying in the 1980s. Mostly, bullying was seen as a way to toughen boys and girls, rather than a poisonous practice as it is rightly understood today.

## Strange and Normal

Reading Eleven's weirdness against the grain, we observe a parallel in the kids' minds between the strange abilities of this girl and the superpowers of a comic-book superhero. In the beginning, Mike believes that the group should conceive their own freakiness in terms of superpowers, an advantage rather than a deficiency.

Heroism and freakiness run in parallel throughout *Stranger Things*. Eleven, a somewhat freakish teenager who violates the laws and the labels (male/female, normal/abnormal, human/monster) is also a hero after rescuing her friends and terminating the other monster. In fact, the abnormal (hysterical Joyce, queer male kids, androgynous

Eleven, shy Barb) are the heroes. *Stranger Things* jumps ahead to the new millennium, where difference is celebrated ("Holly, Jolly"):

> **LUCAS:** She's not a superhero, She's a weirdo.
>
> **MIKE:** Why does that matter? The X-men are weirdos.

# 16
# Gotta Have Faith

ANDREW M. WINTERS

An orange glow illuminates Eleven's bloodied face. Here at the gate to the Upside Down she confronts a shadow reminiscent of H.R. Giger's *Alien*, lurking behind a luminescent fibrous wall. With anticipation, we watch as she attempts to close the gate, to seal the Upside Down from the town of Hawkins.

The hope is that Will will no longer be possessed and that things in the quaint town of Hawkins may return to somewhat of a semblance of normalcy. We have faith in El that she will succeed. Her friends have faith that she will succeed. El has faith in herself that she will succeed as she channels her anger to combat the shadow that lurks behind the gate. Although we, along with Eleven and her friends, clearly have faith that she will succeed, it is not clear what faith *is*.

"The Gate" brings Season Two of *Stranger Things* to a climactic point in which we see the tests of faith in various forms—the test of faith in our friends, families, and ourselves. This kind of faith is not too different from the sort of faith that many of us have in the *transcendent* (that which is not immanent), including the divine, the future, or love. We orient our lives to align with the things in which we have faith.

For those of us who have faith in a god, we orient ourselves to conform to the moral codes and ideals that will ensure we meet the conditions for the desirable afterlife. When we have faith in the future, we make decisions that will allow us to become who we wish to be. As for love, when we experience love (and not just lust) we take risks to pursue projects that will allow those loving relationships to flourish. For these reasons, like the characters in *Stranger Things*, by having faith we take risks that give our lives meaning.

## Faith in the Future, Others, and Ourselves

At the end of the first season of *Stranger Things*, Eleven's friends presume that she has disappeared. Despite this presumption, they have faith that she will return. While Mike, Lucas, Will, and Dustin are swept up in their game of Dungeons & Dragons, there appears to be an unspoken understanding that they all miss Eleven. Yet, Mike's basement is still setup with Eleven's hideaway from the final episode of Season One ("The Upside Down"). Hopper has faith that he will find Eleven as he sets out traps baited with Eggos. Not only was Eleven the Mage of their group, although we are still waiting for her to play a campaign of D&D, she helped them understand the Upside Down and how to defeat the Demogorgon that attacked them in the school.

Because of their close ties and what they went through, the members of the Party are unwilling to give up on the possibility that Eleven might return. There is no evidence available to them, though, that she will return. At best, they can only appeal to their faith that she is not gone and that at some time in the future she rejoins the Party. Like many of us, the Party members have faith that the future will be different, and perhaps even better, than the present.

When Eleven sets out to fight the Mind Flayer at the end of Season Two, there appear to be at least two expressions of faith. First, because Eleven has faith in herself she believes herself capable of defeating the Mind Flayer and closing the gate. She reflects on her previous abilities in successfully defeating the Demogorgon, flipping vans, and crushing the brain of Connie Frazier (along with other government workers), having done so using only her biokenesis. So, while Eleven is rightfully confident in using her powers against threats, she has yet to encounter something as threatening as the Mind Flayer. Her faith in herself, however, allows her to confidently assert that she will defeat the Mind Flayer and close the gate.

The second form of faith when Eleven sets out to fight the Mind Flayer occurs among her friends. It's because of their faith in Eleven's abilities that they are willing to take on a range of personal risks. Among these risks include the scorching of the slimy, and seemingly telepathic, roots that connect the Upside Down to the town of Hawkins. In doing so, they lure a pack of demodogs to their own location. In case it's not already obvious why these actions are risky, let's look at them one at a time.

First, we all know that we shouldn't play with fire—let alone engulf an enclosed area with flammable liquids and then strike a match. Second, luring demodogs is dangerous. We saw what they're capable of doing to cats (poor Mews) and humans (poor Bob). So, Dustin thinking that it would be a good idea to lure demodogs to their immediate location is a thought that should be quickly dismissed (sorry, buddy). If anything, *Stranger Things* should be fraught with "Don't try this at home" warnings. But, Eleven's friends *are* willing to risk immolation and becoming demodog treats. Their faith leads them to take risks that end up paying off big and making for an excellent viewing experience (I'm sure that I wasn't the only person yelling at the screen "Get out!"). So, while it's clear what the risk may be in ensuring that Eleven is successful in closing the gate to the Upside Down, it remains unclear what their faith is that allows her friends to take on such exorbitant risks.

## Gotta Have Faith but Don't Gotta Have Religion

When we think about the concept of *faith* we are most likely to correlate the concept to religious objects, images, and symbols. You know, crosses, prayers, and angels . . . those sorts of things. If not, well, these are the sorts of things that come to *my* mind when I hear someone utter the word "faith." This also seems to be the case for other philosophers. Most philosophers who have done work on the nature of faith have approached faith from a religious perspective. John Hick's 1967 entry on "Faith" in *The Encyclopedia of Philosophy* provides an excellent account of how faith has shown up in both Catholic and Protestant thought. He then covers how philosophical figures such as Pascal, James, and Tennant explore the concept—as it turns out, though, each of them discusses faith as it occurs within religious practice. Even the later discussions in Hick's entry on the relationship between faith and freedom and how faith should be interpreted are done from within a religious framework. This substantive discussion on the issue, especially in something like *The Encyclopedia of Philosophy*, would make it seem that you must be religious to have faith. Well, this is just not true. Hear me out.

Perhaps an odd source for philosophical reflection is 1980s pop music, which brings me to the second thing that comes to my mind when I hear someone say the word "faith," George Michael's 1987 song "Faith." (Please, pretty please, if you have no idea what I'm referring to, do a quick Google search—you'll either thank me or hate me. If you know what I'm talking about, go ahead and look it up anyway—you deserve a treat for having read this far.) While George Michael famously dons a dangling cross earing in the music video (remember those things? Music videos—not dangling ear rings), he was most likely not thinking about Jesus when he sang, "Well, I guess it would be nice if I could touch your body / I know not everybody has got a body like you." Why would he be using a word like 'faith' to refer to his desire to touch someone's body? It certainly isn't a prayer . . . well, maybe, but not a prayer in the traditional religious sense. It's tied to his desire to come into contact with the transcendent . . . something akin to beauty.

Similarly, the members of the Party were not concerned with religious aspects of faith when they permitted themselves to become demodog bait. They didn't bring with them any religious talisman; there was no utterance of prayer before setting foot into the tunnels; and there was no instance at which Dustin raises The Holy Bible in front of a demodog shouting "The power of Christ compels you!" Nope, instead they brought snorkel gear, gasoline, and a badass-can-do attitude reminiscent of Eighties flicks like *The Goonies*. Yet, it was their faith in Eleven and their own abilities to assist her that led them to take on those risks—nothing dealing with religion.

So, I acknowledge that our initial intuitive approach to offering an account of faith would involve evoking something religious. But intuitions are often wrong (for example, our intuitions maintain that Earth is at the center of the universe, but it's not . . . sorry, geocentrists, and thank you, science). Both George Michael and the members of the Party provide us with intuitive reasons for thinking that there is not a necessary connection between faith and religion. In other words, it is possible that we can have faith without being religiously inclined. This may be a relief for some of us, but it still doesn't tell us what faith *is*.

## Faith in Philosophy

One of my favorite questions to ask when doing philosophy is: *Why should I care?* It's especially great when one of my students asks this question—it provides me with an opportunity to explain the importance of the investigation underway. So, in the case of understanding the nature of faith, we can ask *Why should I care about understanding faith—especially if I'm not religious?*

I claim that what we have faith *in* shapes our behaviors with regards to that thing. If the members of the party did not have faith in their friend Eleven's capabilities to close the gate, then it is highly unlikely that they would have exposed themselves to such risks as a pack of demodogs. I recognize that they're kids and that kids often expose themselves to unnecessary risks (as if adults don't also do this), but these kids are frickin' smart. Let's give them some credit. They are members of the A/V Club, after all.

So, maybe the young adolescents of *Stranger Things* aren't enough to sway you that we should care about faith. Perhaps this line of reasoning will instead move you to care. In our own individual lives, our faith determines the risks we're willing to take. If we did not have faith that at least some things will work out (when we don't have clear evidence that those things *will* work out), then it is highly unlikely that we would take any risks. But, it's because of the risks that we take that we have the capacity to live meaningful lives—a life that is not just mediocre or complacent. So, if it is the case that religion is not the sole source of faith and faith has the capacity to shape the kinds of lives we live, then we had better figure out what faith is. Thank goodness for philosophy. Okay, I admit, philosophy is not the easiest route to figuring something out. But, when you discover something as a result of philosophical reflection, you know that you have better reasons for holding onto the belief than if you had flipped a coin or simply listened to your parents (sorry, Mom and Dad).

## Faithful Models

Philosophers continue to discuss the nature of faith after Hick's 1967 entry. Due to philosophers having gotten their analytic tools on this concept, however, there is little agreement on what faith is. (I know, it's shocking that philosophers would disagree.) It's true that much of the discussion has focused on theistic (or religious) faith, even Bishop's 2016 entry "Faith" in the *Stanford Encyclopedia of Philosophy* is from a religious perspective. Given that we do not have to think of faith from a religious perspective, thanks to the members of the Party and George Michael having shown us the way, I've reframed Bishop's models to accommodate a secular approach (I think Dustin would approve; yes, he's my favorite member of the Party).

Some of the candidate models are that faith involves a feeling (*purely affective model*); knowledge that is acquired by something transcendent (*special knowledge model*); belief that something transcendent exists (*belief model*); trust in something transcendent (*trust model*); practical commitment to something beyond the readily available evidence (*doxastic venture model*); practical commitment to something without believing in it (*non-doxastic venture model*); and acting in accordance with the way you hope something is (*hope model*). We're not going to try and figure out which model of faith is the accurate one, although I do have my favorites. Instead, let's see which model might be best fitting to what happens in the last episode of Season Two of *Stranger Things*.

On the purely affective model, a person has existential confidence. This confidence can involve faith that something exists and that the thing in question has particular attributes. In the case of *Stranger Things*, we see that Eleven believes that she exists (she says "I") and she has the feeling of confidence that she is capable of closing the gate. We also see the members of the party maintaining a similar feeling with regards to their own abilities to assist Eleven and Eleven's capacity to defeat the Mind Flayer. So, the affective model holds.

On the special knowledge model, a person has knowledge of specific truths as revealed by the thing that a person has faith in. This, however, does not hold for the party. It is not because of the Mind Flayer, the Demogorgon, or Eleven that they come to know the specific truth that Eleven should close the gate. Instead, it is something that they've come to infer as a result of the readily available evidence. So, sorry special knowledge model . . . it's not your day.

We have similar reasons for thinking that the belief, trust, doxastic venture, and non-doxastic venture models are not applicable to the party's willingness to take the risks that they do to assist Eleven close the gate. On the belief model, it would involve them having faith that something like the Mind Flayer exists. But they don't have to just have faith that it exists—they saw what it did to their friend Will Byers. For them to not believe that the Mind Flayer exists would be just plain cruel. The trust model doesn't work because there is nothing for them to trust or believe in that is not immediately present. Demogorgons, Mind Flayers, Eleven . . . they're all there. To not trust their senses would be inconsistent with their other actions. The doxastic (a fancy word for 'belief') venture model would require having a practical commitment beyond the available evidence that a particular entity exists. But, similar to the reasons for rejecting the other models, the party members have all the evidence they need. They don't need to venture beyond to claim that the things attacking them exist. Last, the non-doxastic venture model would need the party members to not believe that something like the Mind Flayer exists but still claim that claims about the Mind Flayer are true. Given that their actions are in accordance with the belief that the Mind Flayer exists (why else would they try to help Eleven destroy it?), it is more likely that they believe that the Mind Flayer does exist. So, goodbye non-doxastic venture model (you didn't make sense anyway).

While the theistic interpretation of the hope model has someone acting in accordance with the hope that something like God exists, we can adopt a secular interpretation of the hope model. Instead of thinking that God exists, we can have hope in those things that are not immediately present (such as the future), each other (in the way that the party members have hope in Eleven's abilities), and ourselves (in the way that Eleven has faith in her own abilities to defeat the Mind Flayer). Yes, I know that I said that the purely affective model also applies (I didn't forget), but I've said everything I care to say about feelings. Let's talk about hope instead.

## Faith and the Future

We have faith (as hope) that the future will exist. We don't have any immediate evidence that the future will occur, yet we live as if it will occur. We really can't do anything else. The hope we have about the future, however, is really about the possibility of present causes producing future effects. In other words, we have faith that causation will continue to work as it has in the past. What would be the justification for this kind of hope?

Probably one of my favorite philosophers, David Hume (1711–1776) had spent some time thinking about the nature of causation. In his *Enquiry Concerning Human Understanding* (1748), he helped us understand how causation is something we do not directly observe. (Really, try to observe causes.) At best, he suggested, we can only observe one event being followed by the other. When two events are observed following in sequence on a regular basis, then we maintain that the earlier event is the cause of the second event. But there is no observational evidence to justify the one event being the cause of the second. Instead, we come to believe as a matter of custom or habit (or, *cough*, faith) that the causal regularities hold. This habit allows us to have hope that by doing some particular actions that we will produce the particular desirable effects.

Don't despair, though. Even though we don't have good reasons for thinking that one event causes the other, we should continue living for pragmatic reasons. And this is the very sort of thing that Hume would recommend to the members of the Party—don't stop eating Eggos just because you don't have good reasons for believing that they will nourish you (well, you probably don't have any reasons for *that*). But don't stop eating…the risk is just to high. Keep the hope that food will nourish until given good reasons for not having that hope. These beliefs seem to make intuitive sense, and without evidence to the contrary (what philosophers call *defeaters*), keep believing it even if you don't have reasons to support the belief. In other words, don't think about causation too hard.

We see the members of the Party at various points throughout *Stranger Things* employ this kind of faith (as hope) to produce desirable future effects. For example, when heat is used in Season Two to draw the Mind Flayer out of Will Byers ("The Gate"), the hope is that heat will have the effect of removing the Mind Flayer from Will. In Season One, Eleven uses a kiddie pool filled with 1,500 pounds of salt and water to create a mock sensory deprivation tank ("The Bathtub"). The hope is that by having Eleven placed in the pool, she will be able to find Will or Barb (sorry, Barb).

Earlier in Season One, Joyce Byers strung Christmas lights that corresponded to letters in hopes that Will could communicate to her ("Holly, Jolly"). Without having the hope that these particular actions would not generate the desired effect, none of those actions would have been performed. But these are good things for the party, Joyce, and Hopper to have done—even if they didn't have direct evidence for doing so. They performed those actions because they had faith in causation and the future, indicating that faith might be a good thing. And if George Michael's song "Faith" is no longer stuck in your head, it should be now . . . "Cause I gotta have faith . . ." Did I *cause* you to think about the song? I hope so.

## Faithful Relations

In addition to having faith in causal relations we have faith in personal relations. Among the most significant and emotionally intense relationships are loving relationships. In large part, it's due to the associated risks with love that makes these kinds of relationships so significant. I won't get too far into the concept of *love*, but you can be sure that philosophers are also not in agreement as to what love is. There's even an entire society dedicated to the philosophical study of sex and love (The Society for the Philosophy of Sex and Love; yes, I'm a member).

What I will share, though, is that the Early Greeks offer a model of the different kinds of love that some of us are fortunate enough to experience (and, yes, I'm assuming that love is a good thing—despite its intensity and associated risks). There are, of course, discussions about the extent to which these are distinct or related to one another, but it's a good starting point for thinking about our relationships.

There are three main forms of love *eros, philia,* and *agape* with which the Early Greeks concerned themselves. We see all three forms of love showing up in *Stranger Things*. Eros is the passionate desire for an object and is typically expressed sexually. For example, in Season One eros is certainly in effect when Nancy and Steven are alone in his room as Barb waits by the pool ("The Weirdo on Maple Street"). Philia is the form of affection we feel for friends and family members, which we see being expressed in Season Two between Will and his brother, Jonathan, as they discuss what it means to be a freak in light of Will's new nickname "Zombie Boy" ("Trick or Treat, Freak"), or in Season One when they're listening to the Clash ("The Weirdo on Maple Street"). Agape, however, is a little trickier to explain. My preferred understanding of agape is that it is expressed when we acknowledge that each person has intrinsic value similar to the value that we bestow upon ourselves. It's what allows us to feel a connection to others whom we have never met, or to have the sense that what we're experiencing is akin to what someone else must be experiencing. Agape is expressed when the townspeople of Hawkins bring Joyce a casserole or go on the search for Will when he goes missing ("The Vanishing of Will Byers").

In each of these forms of love, though, we can see that faith (or hope) is tied to the relationship. Nancy and Steven certainly have hope that they'll experience pleasure (if you don't understand what I mean, talk to your parents), but also that their desire for one another will be reciprocated. Will and Jonathan hope that they can trust one another and find comfort in each other's company. Last, the townspeople hope that they can find Will and assuage Nancy's fears. In all three of these scenarios, there is no direct evidence indicating that what they have hope in will come to fruition. Instead, it is purely based on them having faith in their relationships with each other that they see it worthwhile to take on the risks of loving each other—whatever form love may take.

## Faith in Ourselves

When Eleven successfully defeats the Mind Flayer, closing the gate and causing a slew of demodogs to fall to the pits, she collapses from exhaustion—but there's a look of relief on her face. Haven't you experienced something similar (okay, not *that* similar), but some experience where you surprised yourself? Perhaps you had taken a risk to do something you did not know was going to work out, but you knew that if you didn't at least try then you'd never know if you could do that thing. Sometimes things do work out. What leads us to try?

Eleven very well could have failed. The Mind Flayer is brutal. Eleven had to use the memory of every horrible experience she had as a source of anger to muster the strength needed to send the Mind Flayer behind the gate. Yet, had she not even attempted, then Hawkins and the world would be enslaved by Demogorgon overlords—if they even wanted to keep us around. So, what led her to try?

Unsurprisingly, we can appeal to faith as the source of inspiration to try the things that we might fail at doing, but know that we need to do those things. (This includes living a meaningful life.) At some point, we become aware of what we should do—not so much because of the act itself, but because of how the action is aligned with some higher ideal or goal.

In his 1843 book *Fear and Trembling*, Søren Kierkegaard understood these actions in terms of the (wait for it) *teleological suspension of the ethical*. This is where the ethical itself is no longer a goal in itself, but the ethical is subservient to some other end or purpose. So, we would no longer be able to say that an action should be performed because it is ethical. Instead, we would say that we should perform some action because it is ethical and in doing something ethical we are fulfilling some higher purpose.

By maintaining this kind of attitude towards our actions we bring purpose into our own lives, but it also allows for some justification of sacrifice. Eleven knew that her purpose was to close the gate, but more importantly to protect her friends and to save the world from the Upside Down. She believed that she was the one responsible for bringing the Upside Down to Hawkins, so she felt a responsibility to rectify the situation. In attempting to do so, she could have very well failed, but she could have also died in the process of succeeding. She knew that the sacrifice would've been worth it, since it would've been in accordance with that higher ideal. In this case, that ideal would be friendship. It is in having done the unthinkable, though, that Eleven was able to live a life that was worth living. What might we learn from her?

By aligning our lives with some purpose or goal we can begin cultivating the faith needed to pursue that goal. It is very well possible that we may fail, but given that our lives are defined in terms of that greater purpose, we can then take the risk of living a meaningful life. For Kierkegaard, this is exactly what faith is—the paradox of aligning an individual with something universal. In other words, faith is what allows us to move beyond ourselves. This is something that is unthinkable, hence "paradox," but it is when we do the unthinkable that our lives have the most meaning.

What kind of person is capable of living this kind of life? Kierkegaard refers to this person as the *knight of faith*. Not only does the knight of faith strive to overcome pain and hardships, but she also persists even when the situation appears absurd. It is in the willingness to overcome the absurd that faith is realized. It is to acknowledge both the impossibility of the situation and to not accept the impossibility. Otherwise, there would be no need for faith.

This is the case for Eleven. She knows that it is absurd for an adolescent woman to overcome the Mind Flayer. Yet, she refuses to accept the absurdity, knowing that to not at least attempt to overcome the absurdity would render her life meaningless. Faith is the very thing that allows her to have the confidence to try in spite of evidence to the contrary—it is the hope that perhaps she will be successful. Her dilemma is either to not attempt and guarantee that she lives a meaningless life (since she would not be aligning her life with her purpose) or to attempt the act and take a chance that either she will succeed or die trying (in either case her life would be aligned with her greater purpose). So, when we are presented with a similar dilemma we can either choose to align ourselves with some purpose or not. Ultimately, the choice becomes either to have a meaningful life or not. For those of us who choose to align our lives with something meaningful, something beyond our individual selves, we must look beyond what is immediately presented to us and not give in to the absrd—we must have faith.

## Faith and Meaning

Similar to having a mistakenly religious understanding of faith, we may come to think that to have faith in ourselves involves rejecting reason and the world. Kierkegaard maintains that this is not the case (p. 77). In having faith to attempt to pursue the infinite, the goals that are beyond our individual selves, we must accept everything that is presented to us. Through faith we have hope, and with this hope we are able to develop courage. It is this very faith that served as the basis of Eleven's heroic efforts to conquer the Mind Flayer. May we follow her lead and conquer our own fears that stand in the way of us living in accordance with our purpose.

It's when we have this kind of courage that we're willing to take on projects that will impact the future. When we have hope that results in courage, we are able to enter into loving relationships with others. And it is when we have courage that we are able to become the people we wish to become, or we take ourselves to already be (and afraid to share with the world). These are the very things, though, that give our lives meaning—the future, our relationships, and authenticity. For these reasons, we can begin seeing how by having faith we can live more meaningful lives. It worked out for Eleven and the other members of the Party, it might just work out for us.[1]

---

[1] For Lindsay. Thank you.

# Bibliography

Aristotle. 2014. *Aristotle: Nicomachean Ethics*. Cambridge University Press.

Augustine. 1998. *Augustine: The City of God Against the Pagans*. Cambridge University Press.

Baudrillard, Jean. 1994. *Simulacra and Simulation*. University of Michigan Press.

Becker, Ernest. 2018 [1973]. *The Denial of Death*. Souvenir Press.

Bentham, Jeremy. 1948 [178]. *An Introduction to the Principles of Morals and Legislation*. Hafner.

Bishop, John. 2016. Faith. *The Stanford Encyclopedia of Philosophy*. <https://plato.stanford.edu/archives/win2016/entries/faith/>.

Bradley, Laura. 2017. How Stranger Things Season 2 Brought Justice for Barb. *Vanity Fair* (October 26th). <www.vanityfair.com/hollywood/2017/10/stranger-things-season-2-barb-story-justice-for-barb-what-happened-to-barb>.

Burton, Neel L. 2012. *Hide and Seek: The Psychology of Self-Deception*. Acheron.

Campbell, Joseph. 1973 [1949]. *The Hero with a Thousand Faces*. Princeton University Press.

Canguilhem, Georges. 1962. La Monstruosité et le Monstrueux. *Diogène* 40:29.

Capelouto, J.D. 2016. This Malden Vigil for a "Stranger Things" Character Has over 1,000 RSVPs. Boston.com (August). <www.boston.com/news/local-news/2016/08/15/this-malden-vigil-for-a-stranger-things-character-has-over-1000-rsvps>.

Carroll, Noël. 2003. *The Philosophy of Horror: Or, Paradoxes of the Heart*. Routledge, 2003.

Chaney, Jen. 2017. The Duffer Brothers Recap Stranger Things 2, "Chapter Three: The Pollywog". *Vulture* (November). <www.vulture.com/2017/11/duffer-brothers-recap-stranger-things-2-the-pollywog.html>.

Cook, Alissa Michelle. 2013. Of Memory and Muses: The Wellsprings of Creativity. PhD dissertation, Montana State University—Bozeman, College of Letters and Science.

Cornford, Francis MacDonald. 2014. *Plato's Cosmology: The Timaeus of Plato*. Routledge.

Darwin, Charles. 1871. *The Descent of Man, and Selection in Relation to Sex*. John Murray.

Derrida, Jacques. 2005 [1997]. The *Politics of Friendship*. Verso.

Dewey, John. 1998. *The Essential Dewey: Pragmatism, Education, Democracy*. Volume 1. Indiana University Press.

Didi-Huberman, Georges. 2000. *Devant le Temps: Histoire de l'Art et Anachronisme des Images*. Editions de Minuit.

———. 2005. *Confronting Images: Questioning the Ends of a Certain History of Art*. Pennsylvania State University Press.

Durant, William James. 1958. *The Story of Philosophy: The Lives and Opinions of the World's Greatest Philosophers from Plato to John Dewey*. Pocket Books.

Feagin, Susan L. 1983. The Pleasures of Tragedy. *American Philosophical Quarterly* 20:1.

Forgotten Realms Wiki. 2019. Mind Flayer. <https://forgottenrealms.fandom.com/wiki/Mind_flayer>.

Foucault, Michel. 2003. *Abnormal: Lectures at the Collège de France, 1974–1975*. Picador.

Getz, D. Stranger Things: New York Pizzeria Now Serves Special Barb Slices. EW.com. <https://ew.com/article/2016/08/03/stranger-things-barb-pizza>.

Gilligan, Carol. 2014. Moral Injury and the Ethic of Care: Reframing the Conversation about Differences. *Journal of Social Philosophy* 45:1.

Gilovich, T., J. Kruger, V.H. Medvec, K. Savitsky, P. Bryant, M.B. Salwen, and M. Dupagne. 2012. The Spotlight Effect—You are Not So Smart: Why Your Memory Is Mostly Fiction, Why You Have Too Many Friends on Facebook and 46 Other Ways You're Deluding Yourself 78:2.

Grater, Tom. 2017. Emmys 2017: The Duffer Brothers Talk "Stranger Things". *Screen*. <www.screendaily.com/features/emmys-2017-the-duffer-brothers-talk-stranger-things/5119204.article?referrer=RSS.

Heidegger, Martin. 1996 [1927]. *Being and Time: A Translation of Sein und Zeit*. SUNY Press.

Hick, John. 1967. Faith. In Paul Edwards, ed., *The Encyclopedia of Philosophy*. Macmillan.

History.com, editors. 2017. MK-Ultra. History.com. <https://www.history.com/topics/us-government/history-of-mk-ultra>.

Holme, Adrian. 2019. A House Built on Sand? A Critical Examination of the Concept of "Identity" within Contemporary "Identity Politics," from a Sociological Perspective. *Interalia*.

Hume, David. 1988 [1748]. *An Enquiry Concerning Human Understanding*. Open Court.

James, William, Frederick Burkhardt, and H.S. Thayer. 1975. *Pragmatism*. Volume 1. Harvard University Press.

Jung, Carl Gustav. 2014. *Aion: Researches into the Phenomenology of the Self*. Routledge.

Kieran, Matthew. 2004. *Revealing Art*. Routledge.

Kierkegaard, Søren. 2013. *Kierkegaard's Writings, VI, Volume 6: Fear and Trembling / Repetition*. Princeton University Press.

King, Stephen. 1993. Interview with Charlie Rose. <charlierose.com/videos/16779>.

Kolnai, Aurel. 2004 [1927]. *On Disgust*. Open Court.

Kimmel, Jimmy. 2018. Shannon Purser on the Barb/Stranger Things Phenomenon. *Jimmy Kimmel Live* <www.youtube.com/watch?v=3B4UzJOLhtc>.

Locke, John. 1996 [1668] *An Essay Concerning Human Understanding*. Hackett.

Louden, Bruce. 2011 *Homer's Odyssey and the Near East*. Cambridge University Press.

Mead, George Herbert. 1934. *Mind, Self, and Society*. University of Chicago Press.

Meyer, Marvin, ed. 2010. *The Nag Hammadi Scriptures: The Revised and Updated Translation of Sacred Gnostic Texts*. Harper.

Muir, Juliet. 2018. Remains Identified as Missing 27-year-old Mother Jamie Haggard. NBCNews.com. <www.nbcnews.com/feature/cold-case-spotlight/remains-identified-missing-27-year-old-mother-jamie-haggard-n893366>.

Nietzsche, Friedrich Wilhelm. 1974. *The Gay Science: With a Prelude in German Rhymes and an Appendix of Songs*. Vintage.
———. 1986 [1878]. *Human, All Too Human*. Cambridge University Press.
Noddings, Nel. 2003. *Caring: A Feminine Approach to Ethics and Moral Education*. University of California Press.
Nuzzo, Luciano. 2013. Foucault and the Enigma of the Monster. *International Journal for the Semiotics of Law / Revue Internationale de Sémiotique Juridique* 26:1.
Padva, Gilad. 2014. *Queer Nostalgia in Cinema and Pop Culture*. Springer.
Plato. 1997. *Plato: Complete Works*. Hackett.
———. 2016. *The Republic of Plato*. Basic Books.
Pomeroy, Ross. 2014. A Psychiatric Evaluation of Michael Myers. *RealClearScience*. <www.realclearscience.com/blog/2014/10/a_psychiatric_evaluation_of_michael_myers.html>.
Quispel, Gilles. 1980. Valentinian Gnosis and the Apocryphon of John. In *The Rediscovery of Gnosticism*. Brill.
Reddit. 2019. R/StrangerThings—Graffiti Found in LA. <www.reddit.com/r/StrangerThings/comments/4tz9nn/graffiti_found_in_la>.
Regan, Tom. 2004. *The Case for Animal Rights*. University of California Press.
Reilly, Kaitlin. 2019. "Riverdale" Just Threatened to Kill Off Barb Again Which Is Like, The Opposite of Justice. Riverdale Season 2 Spoilers Ethel Muggs Dies, Barb. <www.refinery29.com/en-us/2017/10/178057/riverdale-ethel-muggs-dies-shannon-purser-barb-stranger-things>.
Ryder, Richard D. 1970. *Speciesism, Painism, and Happiness: A Morality for the 21st Century*. Imprint Academic.
Sacks, Oliver. 1985. The Lost Mariner. In *The Man Who Mistook His Wife for a Hat*.
Sharpe, Andrew. 2007. Foucault's Monsters, the Abnormal Individual, and the Challenge of English Law. *Journal of Historical Sociology* 20:3.
Singer, Peter. 1995 [1975]. *Animal Liberation*. Random House.
Starobinski, Jean, and William S. Kemp. 1966. The Idea of Nostalgia. *Diogenes* 14:54.
Steward, Susan. 1992. *On Longing: Narratives of the Miniature, the Gigantic, the Souvenir, the Collection*. Duke University Press.

# Bibliography

Sutton, John. 2004. Memory. *Stanford Encyclopedia of Philosophy*. <https://stanford.library.sydney.edu.au/archives/fall2006/entries/memory>.

Tobias, S. 2016. A Stranger Things Glossary: Every Major Film Reference in the Show, from A–Z. *Vulture* (July). <https://www.vulture.com/2016/07/stranger-things-film-reference-glossary.html>.

# The Party

FRANKLIN S. ALLAIRE (@misterallaire on Twitter) is an Assistant Professor of Science Education at the University of Houston—Downtown. A self-proclaimed "stand-up philosopher," he has previously contributed chapters to *The Walking Dead and Philosophy* and *Jeopardy! and Philosophy*. His research interests include the construction, intersection, and maintenance of identity and issues impacting the success of underrepresented minorities in STEM. If he had any special powers like Eleven, Franklin swears he would use them for good and occasionally revenge against Reviewer #2 and robocallers.

ADAM BARKMAN is Professor of Philosophy and Chair of the philosophy department at Redeemer University College (Canada). He is the author and editor of a dozen books, including *Making Sense of Islamic Art and Architecture* (2015) and *The Philosophy of Ang Lee* (2013). He is also the co-editor of Lexington's Critical Companion to Contemporary Directors series, which includes his newest book, *A Critical Companion to Steven Spielberg* (2019).

COLE BOWMAN is a writer and independent scholar located in Portland, Oregon. She has contributed chapters to other Popular Culture and Philosophy volumes including *The Ultimate Walking Dead and Philosophy*, *Dracula and Philosophy*, *Dr. Who and Philosophy*, and *Star Wars and Philosophy*. She's also written several pieces for the Things from Another World Comics website.

**JEREMY CHRISTENSEN** is an Instructor of Communication at Davis & Elkins College in Elkins, West Virginia, where he coaches the debate team and teaches courses in public address, rhetoric, as well as in communication and culture. His research interests are in the twentieth-century novel and involve the study of nostalgia informed by the work of Michel Foucault and Jean Baudrillard. His greatest interest, however, is his three children, who also have been informed by Foucault and Baudrillard, a sort of academic collateral damage during several of their father's road trip lectures. As his daughter remarked and sons concurred upon discovering their dad was writing a chapter for the book: "Daddy, the show doesn't hold a candle to you; I can't imagine anything stranger than something you would write."

**DANIEL CORNELL** completed his undergraduate degree in Philosophy at University College London and then completed a Masters in Philosophy at The University of St. Andrews with a particular interest in early analytic philosophy. The late American Philosopher W.V. Quine once quipped that philosophers fall into two camps; those who are interested in the history of philosophy, and those who are interested in philosophy. Daniel falls into the former camp with a recent interest landing upon early twentieth-century psychoanalysis.

**JEFF EWING** loves *Stranger Things* but he can't help falling down random-thought rabbit trails, like: *if the Upside Down is a derivative copy of our dimension, is there a derivative copy of IT? And a copy of that one? Where does it stop? (Or are we a copy of the Upside Down that got carried away with itself?) And what if the fine folks at Eggo are in on the government conspiracy?* \*ahem\* For Season Three he's hoping to just watch and enjoy the show . . . You can find Jeff's chapters in other Popular Culture and Philosophy books, like *Frankenstein and Philosophy* and *Jurassic Park and Philosophy*. He has also co-edited *Alien and Philosophy*.

**DIEGO FORONDA** has an MA in Literature from Universidad de Buenos Aires (UBA)—Facultad de Filosofía y Letras (Argentina). He has contributed chapters to *Representations of the Mother-in-Law in Literature, Film, Drama, and Television*, edited by Jo Parnell and *Gender and Contemporary Horror in Film*, edited by Samantha Holland.

CINDY GORDON is a part-time instructor in Communication Studies at the University of North Texas and a full-time wannabe writer. In the process of slowly and painstakingly writing a novel based on the women in her family, she looks for any opportunity to hone her writing skills, even if no one reads her work. Blessed with a strong sense of curiosity and addicted to learning new things, she is hoping to create a synonym for the word 'dilettante' that carries a positive connotation so she can stop insulting herself. When she's not writing, or thinking about writing, she spends her time reading, gardening, and managing the lives of two golden retrievers and two cats who could probably be famous on Instagram if someone would just take the time to do the work.

ENZO GUERRA is the author of a number of articles, including book chapters on the philosophy of cowboys, Scott Adams's ethics, forgiveness in Aristotle, Avicenna, and Aquinas, and the language problems in *The Handmaid's Tale*.

KYLE A. HAMMONDS is a doctoral student at the University of Oklahoma where he follows Chief Hopper's advice to reserve mornings for coffee and contemplation. The stuff Kyle usually contemplates over that morning coffee includes topics related to his major research area, cross-cultural communication. Pop culture is a pet topic that he enjoys studying from a communication perspective. Sometimes there is so much pop culture and communication stuff to consider that Kyle has to reserve his afternoons for coffee and contemplation as well.

ERIC HOLMES is an instructor of composition at Purdue University Global. A native of Portland, Oregon, his academic interests focus on horror, primarily EC horror comics of the 1950s. He proposed to his wife by calling her on a Saturday night at 10:00 P.M. and asking her "Do you know anything about sensory deprivation tanks, specifically how to build one?"

CHERISE HUNTINGFORD has felt the pull of the subterranean ever since she watched *It*, being way too young to brush off the terror as scarily bad TV. She then spent one summer roaming the local underground waterworks with fellow delinquents, but uncovered not much fun . . . or balloons. So a Bachelor of Arts degree in psychology came to replace literal sloshing through below-the-surface shit (thanks, Freud), as well as writing for a London film magazine, and contributing chapters to *American Horror Story and Philosophy* and *Twin Peaks and Philosophy*. Cherise continues to prefer anything inverted or a tad twisted. She still likes bad TV, but only if it's from the Eighties. Also—Cherise is old enough to remember D&D the first time it was cool. Just sayin'.

ANDREW KUZMA first encountered dark dimensions of the 8-bit, comic book, and John Carpenter-variety. Now he lives and teaches in Milwaukee, Wisconsin, where he continues his quest against evil as an ethicist and only occasionally feeds his daughter Madeleine a triple decker Eggo extravganza.

CLARA NISLEY has taught courses in ethics and political and social philosophy. She has published chapters in *Downton Abbey and Philosophy* (2016), *Iron Man vs. Captain America and Philosophy* (2018), and *The Twilight Zone and Philosophy* (2019). She finds questions on aesthetics and morality stimulating and is fascinated by the grotesque Demogorgon. She hopes to continue her inquiry, while searching for the Upside Down.

WILL PAMERLEAU Despite earning a bachelor's degree in engineering, Bill Pamerleau's fascination with philosophy led him to explore the Upside Down world of an academic philosopher: one where job opportunities look real but are actually devoid of living persons. He managed to land a job anyway and has taught philosophy at the University of Pittsburgh at Greensburg for over a quarter of a century. He is the author of *Existentialist Cinema* and several articles and book chapters in the areas of philosophy of film, pragmatism, and existentialism.

MIKKO M. PUUMALA is a doctoral student in philosophy in University of Turku, Finland. He is writing his PhD dissertation on moral demandingness and climate ethics with the support of the Maj and Tor Nessling Foundation. Mikko wants to do philosophy where the people are. That is, in front of their television sets, having microwave TV-dinners and watching *Stranger Things*. His areas of interest range from evolutionary ethics to superheroes and the ethics of space travel. In a game of Dungeons & Dragons, in the very first episode of *Stranger Things*, he would've cast the protection spell.

CHRIS WIGLEY is a government drone and writer from the heart of Robin Hood country. His writing on popular culture, music, and technology appears frequently in print and online. Chris once worked as Santa Claus and begrudgingly documented his experience at_verymerrylife.co.uk. The tabloids loved it. He is still mastering the art of flinging objects with his mind but hasn't had a nosebleed since puberty.

ANDREW M. WINTERS teaches philosophy and religious studies at Yavapai College in Prescott, Arizona. He's still waiting for someone to plug in the Christmas lights, but has grown used to the cold and dark comforts of the Upside Down. His passion for horror and grindcore keeps the Demogorgon away.

FERNANDO GABRIEL PAGNONI BERNS works as Professor at the Universidad de Buenos Aires (UBA)—Facultad de Filosofía y Letras (Argentina). He teaches courses on international horror film and has published chapters in the books *To See the Saw Movies: Essays on Torture Porn and Post 9/11 Horror*, edited by John Wallis; *Critical Insights: Alfred Hitchcock*, edited by Douglas Cunningham; *Dreamscapes in Italian Cinema,* edited by Francesco Pascuzzi; *Reading Richard Matheson: A Critical Survey*, edited by Cheyenne Mathews; *Gender and Environment in Science Fiction*, edited by Christy Tidwell; and *The Films of Delmer Daves*, edited by Matthew Carter. He has written a book about the Spanish horror TV series *Historias para no Dormir* and edited one on the Frankenstein bicentennial.

ANDREA ZANIN loves monsters—she kind of wishes she was one . . . maybe she is, depending on who you talk to. She also lives in London and was born in the 1980s, which makes her insanely cool. Andrea has a Law degree plus an Honors degree in English Literature for which she graduated cum laude, and has contributed to nine Popular Culture and Philosophy books (including this one)—all peripheral to the amount of time she spends spewing words all over the internet (andreazanin.co.uk) and wishing she could meet the Demogorgon (just one little autograph, pretty please).

MARIANA ZÁRATE got her MA from the Universidad de Buenos Aires (UBA)—Facultad de Filosofía y Letras (Argentina). She has published in *Racism and Gothic: Critical Essays*, edited by Universitas Press; *Bullying in Popular Culture: Essays on Film, Television and Novels*, edited by Abigail Scheg; *Projecting the World: Classical Hollywood, the "Foreign," and Transnational*

*Representations* edited by Russell Meeuf; *Uncovering Stranger Things*, edited by Kevin Wetmore, Jr.; and *The Handmaid's Tale and Philosophy*, edited by Rachel Robison-Greene.

# Index